Cambridge Elements

Elements in Public and Nonprofit Administration
edited by
Robert Christensen
Brigham Young University
Jaclyn Piatak
University of North Carolina at Charlotte
Rosemary O'Leary
University of Kansas

VALUE-BASED GOVERNANCE

Gjalt de Graaf
Vrije Universiteit Amsterdam

Shaftesbury Road, Cambridge CB2 8EA, United Kingdom

One Liberty Plaza, 20th Floor, New York, NY 10006, USA

477 Williamstown Road, Port Melbourne, VIC 3207, Australia

314–321, 3rd Floor, Plot 3, Splendor Forum, Jasola District Centre, New Delhi – 110025, India

103 Penang Road, #05–06/07, Visioncrest Commercial, Singapore 238467

Cambridge University Press is part of Cambridge University Press & Assessment, a department of the University of Cambridge.

We share the University's mission to contribute to society through the pursuit of education, learning and research at the highest international levels of excellence.

www.cambridge.org
Information on this title: www.cambridge.org/9781009621649

DOI: 10.1017/9781009621601

© Gjalt de Graaf 2025

This publication is in copyright. Subject to statutory exception and to the provisions of relevant collective licensing agreements, with the exception of the Creative Commons version the link for which is provided below, no reproduction of any part may take place without the written permission of Cambridge University Press & Assessment.

An online version of this work is published at doi.org/10.1017/9781009621601 under a Creative Commons Open Access license CC-BY-NC-ND 4.0 which permits re-use, distribution and reproduction in any medium for non-commercial purposes providing appropriate credit to the original work is given. You may not distribute derivative works without permission. To view a copy of this license, visit https://creativecommons.org/licenses/by-nc-nd/4.0

When citing this work, please include a reference to the DOI 10.1017/9781009621601

First published 2025

A catalogue record for this publication is available from the British Library

ISBN 978-1-009-62164-9 Hardback
ISBN 978-1-009-62163-2 Paperback
ISSN 2515-4303 (online)
ISSN 2515-429X (print)

Cambridge University Press & Assessment has no responsibility for the persistence or accuracy of URLs for external or third-party internet websites referred to in this publication and does not guarantee that any content on such websites is, or will remain, accurate or appropriate.

For EU product safety concerns, contact us at Calle de José Abascal, 56, 1°, 28003 Madrid, Spain, or email eugpsr@cambridge.org

Value-Based Governance

Elements in Public and Nonprofit Administration

DOI: 10.1017/9781009621601
First published online: December 2025

Gjalt de Graaf
Vrije Universiteit Amsterdam
Author for correspondence: Gjalt de Graaf, g.de.graaf@vu.nl

Abstract: Public governance is inherently normative, so it is important to study the values of public governance – particularly in the present-day context, where, given increasingly differentiated Western public governance, many different values come into play and new value conflicts arise. In this Element, a value-based governance (VBG) perspective is presented. In this perspective, values take center stage as the guiding concept in the theory and practice of public administration and are used as a heuristic to understand and analyze public governance. One section focuses on the advantages and disadvantages of coping strategies used by actors and institutions when dealing with value conflicts. In the final section, the author returns to the practice of public governance: the VBG paradigm entails public governance with normative reasoning. Value-based governance is about bringing the value rationality back in and recognizing intrinsic values. This title is also available as Open Access on Cambridge Core.

Keywords: public values, public governance, value conflict, coping strategies, value-based governance

© Gjalt de Graaf 2025

ISBNs: 9781009621649 (HB), 9781009621632 (PB), 9781009621601 (OC)
ISSNs: 2515-4303 (online), 2515-429X (print)

Contents

1 Values at the Heart of Public Governance ... 1

2 Theoretical Background of the Value-Based Governance Perspective ... 23

3 Empirical Research from a VBG Perspective ... 34

4 Dealing with Value Conflict: Some Coping Strategies ... 41

5 The Value-Based Governance Paradigm ... 49

6 Summary and Conclusions ... 65

References ... 69

1 Values at the Heart of Public Governance

1.1 Introduction

People often liken ethics to the brakes in a car: As soon as you want to accelerate and pick up some speed, an ethicist comes along and puts on the brakes (Februari 2020). Yet, in truth, ethics is more like the car's steering wheel: It guides you to where you want to go. So, with the wrong values in the driver's seat, or if value conflict is not dealt with prudently, things can go horribly wrong in public governance, as we will see.

Public governance is inherently normative, so it is important to study the values of public governance – particularly so in the present-day context. In the increasingly differentiated Western public governance, many different values come into play with new value conflicts arise. In this Element, a value-based governance (VBG) perspective is presented. In the VBG perspective, values take center stage as the guiding concept in the theory and practice of public administration and are used as a heuristic to understand and analyze public governance.

In the rest of this section, the need for a VBG perspective in Public Administration will be further discussed. Section 2 lays the theoretical groundwork of such a perspective and will introduce the epistemology and theoretical framework, as well as look at how values are made manifest.

In the following two sections, the focus is on empirical research from the VBG perspective. Section 3 explains how to conduct research about which (public) values are of importance in Western public governance and which values come into conflict most. A cross-case analysis of five case studies will provide the details.

Section 4 focuses on empirical research on the strategies used by actors and institutions when dealing with value conflicts in public governance. This section also points out the advantages and disadvantages of each of these coping strategies. The same five case studies will be revisited, and a literature review conducted to find the answers.

In Section 5, the contours of VBG in practice are sketched – the VBG paradigm – with suggestions for public governance practice in which scandals such as those described at the beginning of this section are prevented. Section 6 consists of a summary and conclusions.

1.2 Bad Governance

Things can go horribly wrong in public governance. Arguably, the biggest scandal that Dutch public governance has faced in the twenty-first century is the Childcare Benefits Scandal (*toeslagenaffaire*). Between 2013 and 2019, Dutch authorities wrongly accused tens of thousands of parents of making fraudulent benefit claims, requiring them to pay back in their entirety the allowances they had received. In many cases, this amounted to tens of thousands of euros, and this led to broken relationships, years of poverty and fear for some, and jobs being lost. In short, lives were destroyed (Frederik 2021). In addition – according to a recent estimate – 1,675 children were removed from their homes (Koppenjan 2022b: 6). On January 15, 2021, the Dutch coalition government was forced to stand down because of the scandal (only to return on January 10, 2022, in the same composition, after elections).

What went wrong? Let's start with the inherent tension in all benefits schemes between the values of getting the money out *efficiently* to those entitled to it – a public service which should not cost the taxpayer too much – and making sure no fraud is committed – *combating fraud*. People (voters) have strong emotions about not getting money they are lawfully entitled to, but can feel equally strong emotions about other people receiving public money when they shouldn't. No one is against good public service, and no one is against combating fraud, yet these values can conflict in public governance. Once public values are found to be in conflict, some sort of strategy is needed to deal with the conflict. According to Koppenjan (2022b), the childcare benefits scandal was caused by Dutch politicians adopting a policy in which one value – preventing fraud – was paramount at the expense of all other values. A bias strategy, with the bias on combating fraud. A Parliamentary committee that investigated the scandal concluded: "the desire among politicians for the administration of benefits to be carried out efficiently and the wishes of politicians and society at large to prevent fraud resulted in the creation and implementation of legislation that permitted little scope, if any, for taking account of people's individual circumstances, such as administrative errors committed with no ill-intent" (cited in: Ranchordas 2023: 1375).

The concern with combating fraud had its origin in an earlier problem. In the early 2010s, there had been the "Bulgarians scandal." A Bulgarian gang encouraged Bulgarians to register at Dutch addresses and claim false benefits. The Dutch tax authority paid out the benefits before carrying out checks, and by the time they did check, the Bulgarians were back in Bulgaria, and the money could not be reclaimed. There was a (social) media storm about this fraud, and much political outrage and turmoil. The government promised improvements: A special team was formed to crack down on citizens committing fraud. As of January 1, 2014, a very strict anti-fraud law on benefit claims was in place. Both this law and the political climate were clear about what was expected of the administrators of the tax authorities: They were to combat fraud (Frederik 2021:

221). Going along with the legislation was a 25 million euro investment for the tax authorities to hire 200 employees who would apply extra controls (Frederik 2021). The law also stated that every time a benefit claimant made a mistake, the entire amount of benefits would be repayable, and there would be no hardship clause. A new ICT system was installed to conduct checks (Ranchordas and Scarcella 2021). It was this system that, starting in 2013, "mislabeled more than 26,000 parents as fraudsters, with a disproportionate emphasis on citizens with an immigrant background" (Ranchordas and Scarcella 2021: 397). Sometimes parents were singled out by automatic risk selection systems. In those cases, tax officials conducted a manual scrutiny, but they rarely corrected the result from the algorithm (Ranchordas and Scarcella 2021: 398). The effect was of a ruthless and anonymous state (Koppenjan 2022b).

Of course, within the two ministries involved, there were signs that the policy was too harsh. There were accusations that the bias on anti-fraud was leading to maladministration, and that something was going wrong. But neither the signs nor the voices changed the ruthless way in which the policy was applied. For example, on September 2, 2014, a member of the Benefits Management Team within the tax authority emailed the dossiers of citizens for whom the policy had caused "painful outcomes" (Frederik 2021: 69). The team leader observed that he was having difficulty with the fact that he was unable to do anything for these parents. He decided to get legal advice. The lawyers explained to him that everything was legally compliant. The judicial Division of the Dutch Council of State (the Dutch Supreme Court for a number of administrative cases) almost invariably ruled against the parents who appealed.

At some point, there was a concept paper circulating within the Ministry of Social Affairs and Employment that proposed to change the legislation and limit the recovery of benefits. Meanwhile, another benefits fraud case had become prominent in the media. According to Frederik (2021: 78–79), somewhere within the Ministry, administrators would have been aware of the political circumstances and concluded that the timing wasn't right to ease the anti-fraud legislation. Whatever happened, the concept paper never reached the Minister's desk. Frederik (2021: 79): "Courage was lacking among the public administrators to change things without political approval." In practice, the most important objective of the public administrators in the ministries was to protect the Minister (Frederik 2021: 153). That meant that the anti-fraud value remained paramount. That value was considered as the politically mandated choice of democratically elected politicians, a political mandate that public administrators had to fulfill. So, political signals and the idea that there were concomitant value choices were bowed to instead of public service values – process values of governance – and the personal expertise of the administrators.

This was also true of judicial expertise and the judicial branch. "The judicial Division of the Dutch Council of State acknowledged that the judicial system also failed these families, that too much trust had been placed on the actions of public authorities and their procedures, and that too little consideration had been given to the difference between the law and its enforcement" (Ranchordas and Scarcella 2021: 399).

Unfortunately, the Childcare Benefits Scandal is far from unique in Western governance. Australia recently had the so-called Robodebt scandal, and Norway suffered the "Nye Arbeids- og Velferdsetaten" (NAV) scandal (Rouwhorst 2022). Remarkably, all these very recent scandals – in countries highly placed in international good governance rankings – erupted in the social security domain.

"Robodebt" was an Australian government program from 2010 onwards that had the main aim of retrieving overpayments made to social security recipients, 1.7 billion Australian dollars over five years (Whiteford 2021). "Robodebt involved data-matching historic records of benefit payments made to individuals with past income tax returns, identifying discrepancies between these records. It reduced human investigation of the discrepancies, with the calculation of overpayments for many individuals based on a simple algorithm that averaged earnings over the relevant year" (Whiteford 2021: 341). After complaints from many citizens, there were inquiries and investigations leading to a Federal Court Case that ruled the Robodebt program unlawful. There is evidence that for several years the government ignored evidence that the program was unlawful (Whiteford 2021). The program failed to achieve the budgetary savings, and the "government is in the process of paying back more than $1,000 million to more than 400,000 people." Hundreds of thousands of citizens were negatively affected. Just as in the Childcare Benefits Scandal, we see a ruthless, anonymous state with reports of suicide as a result of the program (Whiteford 2021). All of this happened because of the paramount bias on budgetary savings in the program, and all the evidence that other important values were being seriously undermined was simply being ignored.

The NAV scandal is considered the biggest Norwegian welfare scandal ever (Berglund 2020). The NAV made the mistake of following Norwegian rules when punishing benefit recipients who traveled abroad, instead of applying the EU's European Economic Area (EEA) rules, which Norway subscribes to (Berglund 2019). Being part of EEA means that Norwegians can travel to all countries within the EEA and still be eligible for sick pay and some unemployment benefits (Berglund 2020). Yet at least 4,100 Norwegians were denied these benefits after traveling to an EEA country. Just as in the Childcare Benefits Scandal, recipients had to repay benefits they had received earlier, and this meant a large debt for many (Berglund 2020). And – again just as with the Childcare Benefit Scandal and Robodebt – citizens were fined and prosecuted and ended up in jail for having travelled to an EEA country and received illegitimate benefits; lives were ruined. In 2020, a government-appointed committee that investigated the scandal published a report entitled *Blindsonen* (The Blind Zone). The report contains a long list of mistakes. "Regulations were followed in accordance with political signals and what had become standard practice, instead of what the law actually demanded. Fears have also been expressed that public servants will continue to keep quiet about other potential scandals, because of 'a lack of a whistleblowing culture, pulverization of responsibility and a unacceptable lack of proactivity'" (Berglund 2020: 4–5). It is noteworthy that prosecutors and the court upheld NAV's rules for years even though they were illegal – and there were many signs that they were raising questions about the independence of the judicial branch when handling cases from the administrative branch (Berglund 2019: 2). The report identified many responsible parties: The NAV, the Ministry of Labor and Social Affairs, courts, prosecutors, courts and the academic community. The NAV was characterized by the prevention of unlawful benefit claims, the same fraud obsession as in the Childcare Benefits Scandal. "NAV officials consciously or unconsciously wanted to follow politicians' welfare policy, which has long opposed letting NAV clients collect benefits while sitting on a beach in Spain."

In all three policy fiascoes (Bovens and 't Hart 1996), there was a bias in favor of anti-fraud and efficiency, at the expense of several other important values, such as fairness and lawfulness. Value conflicts were not handled prudently. There were unlawful governmental actions, yet for years, many branches of government, including the judiciary, went along (Rouwhorst 2022). The three cases followed the script of *Murder on the Orient Express*: not one, but (almost) all involved policy actors were the perpetrators. Citizens were treated with distrust and suspicion rather than benevolence (De Graaf and Van Asperen 2016). More trust was placed in computer systems and anonymous algorithms than in people (Ranchordas and Scarcella 2021). Administrators "looked up" more to political supervisors and their value direction, than to the process values of governance such as transparency, fairness, and accountability (Rouwhorst 2022), even though one might expect that public administrators would not just be loyal to their political supervisors, but also to society (De Graaf 2011; Frederik 2021). Public servants shouldn't just look upwards but also around. The (social) media played an important role. In the Childcare Benefits Scandal, for example, it was pressure from the media that made the legislator decide to come up with strict anti-fraud laws, just as pressure from the politicians and thus the public administrators kept them in place. The fraud obsession and political climate biased the system toward the prevention of giving out "free money" and unlawful benefits. Things can go horribly wrong in public governance when value conflicts are not prudently dealt with. These cases show that attention must be paid to values.

1.3 A Value-Based Governance Perspective

Not only the decisions involved in the three scandals, but virtually every decision in public governance carries with it normative implications, and yet the attention given to this is minimal – both in Public Administration (PA) in an academic context, and in the practice of public governance (Gawthrop 1998). *All* policies and laws have consequences for people and institutions; they cannot be value neutral. Nor can the process of governance (cf. Rhodes 2007) be value neutral; instrumental values such as transparency, honesty, and integrity play a significant role (De Graaf and Paanakker 2015; Sandel 1996). All of this has significance for the actors involved. Gawthrop (1998: 21) makes this clear:

> First, no public policy, program or operation is value neutral when it is implemented. Second, every public policy, program, and operation has a discernable subjective impact (positive and negative) on the lives of human beings (i.e., citizens). Third, the responsibility for the effects of these impacts rests with those who, by virtue of their professional authority (i.e., accredited competence), are either directly or indirectly involved in the decision-making processes that energize the action pathways from initiation to implementation.

In May 2020 – a few months into the COVID-19 pandemic – the Dutch government introduced a "Covid-dashboard." It displayed all kinds of information – the R-number, the number of positive tests, hospitalizations, and the number of intensive care beds occupied. The idea was that this information would determine the specific lockdown regime of the Netherlands. But there were numbers that were *not* on that dashboard, numbers that could also be relevant to a lockdown policy, such as figures on unemployment, mental health, and learning deficits. Excluding these values from the dashboard is a (moral) choice; a choice with significant consequences. In public governance, choices between conflicting values are constantly being made – if often unconsciously: *Public governance has an intrinsically normative nature* (Beck Jørgensen and Rutgers 2015: 4). "Governance is a values-based activity" (Stewart 2009: 1), yet the value dimension remains in the background, both in the practice of governance as in the discipline that studies it; both in the theory and praxis of public administration the normative nature is mostly disguised.

The objective in these pages is to build a VBG Perspective that brings the values of governance to the fore, and to guide the praxis of governance towards such a VBG. The Element aims to make visible the all-important dimension of value in public governance, while sketching a public governance paradigm in which values take center stage.

In the rest of this section, the main concepts of this Element are introduced and discussed, with support for the claim that governance is inherently normative. From this claim, the importance of studying the values of public governance emerges, and the proposition is put that it is particularly important to study the topic in the present-day context. In increasingly differentiated Western public governance, many different values come into play, with new value conflicts arising. It is suggested that, despite the importance of values in governance and despite recognition that this whole area should be studied and understood, the normativity of governance has seldom taken center stage in the study of Public Administration. Predominantly, the self-image of Public Administration is that of an instrumental discipline, not a normative one: A technocratic management perspective dominates. That is, despite growing interest in public values, scholarly attention to values remains on the periphery of the dominant Public Administration theories. This suggests a need to enrich the field of PA with a VBG perspective, a perspective that takes values as the central concept. This will both give an account of the important normative core of public governance and offer significant possibilities for the exploration of governance. These possibilities are then illustrated, partly by showing how the concept of values trumps that of interest. As the section concludes, an outline of the rest of the Element is presented.

1.4 Main Concepts: Values and Governance

Concepts are the building blocks of social sciences: Their importance can hardly be overstated. After all, as Deleuze and Guattari (1994: 5) put it: "Concepts are not waiting for us ready-made, like heavenly bodies. There is no heaven for concepts. They must be invented, fabricated, or rather created and would be nothing without their creator's signature."

Yet, core concepts such as power or society are also usually troublesome (Rutgers 2019). The central concept of this Element is: *value*. That means trouble. As Klamer (2016: 48) points out: "The concept of value is treacherous. If you decide to embrace the concept, you have been forewarned. Values are not precise and you cannot hold on to them. People do not walk around with values written on their forehead." Stewart (2009: 1): "Values are tricky to capture, changeable and much less robust than the more familiar forces of self-interest." Further, Rutgers (2015: 4) calls value a tricky concept, and points out that the difficulty in providing a substantial definition is not surprising when we look at the concept's history: since the mid-nineteenth century, efforts to establish an encompassing and comprehensive value theory or axiology have failed.

However, despite not having a clear and distinct definition of "value," we should not shy away from using the concept, or even making it the central concept of this discussion. The fact that it is vague is not necessarily problematic in itself (Provis 2007). Many notions that we use perfectly well, like "fish" or "love," are equally vague (Provis 2007: 21). It is not really so surprising that an everyday concept such as value is diffuse in its meaning and lacks an accepted shared definition. Value belongs to the category of "essentially contested concepts," which include many important sociological core concepts, like power, integrity, or public administration.

Despite the warnings, value – and public values – is a (very) useful concept. Rutgers (2015: 11–12):

> There remains an important way in which public values may indeed be a helpful concept; not as a well-defined theoretical concept to guide action, but as a regulative idea (Meynhardt 2009: 204) to help identify important issues. This is similar to John Rohr's use of the concept of regime values as a guide for action for bureaucrats: It is not a theoretical precise concept, but primarily a pedagogical instrument (cf. Rohr 1989: 68; Overeem 2015). In a similar way, public values is used as a heuristic … As a heuristic, public value can assist to put administrative phenomena in a different light, although there is limited clarity regarding the nature of public values themselves it helps avoid focusing on facts as easy, undisputable starting points.

Klamer (2016) is in search of a value-based economy, while here, the quest is to build a VBG perspective. The departure point of both quests is the same: Klamer's conceptualization of values. This is a value-based approach that both supersedes *and* encompasses three distinctive and currently prevalent ways of dealing with values (Klamer 2016: 43):

(1) The *economist's* approach that equates value with price. Economists can provide a price for everything, even if it is not for sale.
(2) The *culturalist's* approach in which value refers to the "qualities of work of art, scientific contributions, organizations, cities, countries and cultures … In the famous characterization by Oscar Wilde: the economist resembles the cynic who knows the price of everything and the value of nothing, and the culturalist the romantic who knows the value of everything and the price of nothing" (Klamer 2016: 44).
(3) *The moral philosophical approach* in which values have a moral connotation, such as benevolence (De Graaf and Van Asperen 2016) or honesty (De Vries 2002).

A value-based approach integrates these three value approaches (Klamer 2016). *Values*, as used here, are *qualities* (De Graaf and Van der Wal 2008). To be more precise: "Values are qualities of actions, goods, practices, people, and social entities that people find good, beneficial, important, useful, beautiful, desirable, constructive, and so forth. Values are personal in the sense that individuals experience them as such and they are social in the sense that they derive their impact from being shared among groups of people" (Klamer 2016: 62). Having defined values as qualities, it is clear that a "value" is not used to describe "what is," but to evaluate something (Rutgers 2019); something – actions, goods, practices, people, social entities – has value in the perception of the observer; something is given a negative or a positive meaning (Rutgers 2015), in particular a positive meaning, as values are about what is desired.

Klamer (2016: 56) distinguishes four domains of values: personal values, social values, societal values, and transcendental or cultural values.

Personal values are the qualities that concern oneself, someone's own individuality. Examples of often-mentioned personal values include health, autonomy, and personal growth.

Social values indicate qualities of human relationships. Friendship is the most obvious example of a social value.

Societal values are about relationships with a large social entity, such as a society. This is the domain that forms the main focus of this Element. The types of value included are *process* values of public governance, such as transparency, lawfulness, or accountability, and *political* values such as peace, justice, solidarity, or sustainability. In political action, societal values are realized. Klamer (2016: 57): "Societal values include cultural values ..., the shared values of a people. When we are considering a group of people in terms of what they share and in what respect they are different from other people, we will identify their shared values as cultural values. Prudence is a value of the Dutch culture, while pioneering is a typical American value."

Transcendental or cultural values are qualities of historical, artistic, and scientific practices. They pertain to something abstract, an ideal. These values include holiness, morality, and beauty (Haidt 2012).

As for the ontology of values: values – including personal values – are socially constructed and determined, and to a high degree shared in a society (De Graaf, Hoenderboom, and Wagenaar 2010; Rutgers 2015); valuing is a socially established phenomenon. Individual values do not precede the social; they are part of a social context.

Some further definitions of terms related to values are useful at this stage. *Norms* are regulations prescribing proper general and situational conduct. *Morals* (morality) are values and norms taken together (De Graaf and Van der

Wal 2008). *Ethics* is usually defined in moral philosophy as the systematic reflection on morality.

Another central concept in the Element is *governance*. If the concept of value is difficult, governance is not much easier. Bovaird and Löffler (2003: 316) state: "There are few terms which are as vague in social science and in practice as 'governance'." Governance has had different meanings attributed to it (see, for example, Kjaer 2004; Van Kersbergen and Van Waarden 2004), but here it is understood as *solving problems*. *Public governance* is the solving of public problems.

Integrity in the context of governance has been defined as (1) being consistent and coherent in principles, values, and action (Montefiori 1999), (2) following regime values and rules (Rohr 1989), and (3) acting in accordance with relevant moral values, norms, and rules (Huberts, Pijl, and Steen 1999; Huberts et al. 2006). In all these definitions, values are central. Based on the third definition, *public governance integrity* is understood here as the quality of governing in accordance with relevant moral values and norms.

Here *societal* values are central, the values of governance (although institutionally shaped public actors play a central role, as we shall see later). As advised by De Vries (2002: 327): "the inclination to behave ethically is not to be seen as an individual trait but rather as a social or cultural trait, in which learning and imitating behavior are crucial." This means that in the empirical parts of this Element, it is not the *personal* values or integrity of public actors (Nieuwenburg 2007) that are central, as they are in almost all empirical studies in administrative ethics (for example, studying whether a politician is corrupt or not). This also implies that the psychological dimension is mostly excluded here (e.g., Fiske and Tetlock 1997).

Public values (e.g., Beck Jørgensen and Bozeman 2007) are located at the societal level; they are societal values. The meaning of societal values here overlaps considerably with the concept of public values. Bozeman and Johnson (2015: 62): "Scholarly discussion about public values is plentiful and has intensified in recent years, particularly in public administration (for an overview, see: Van der Wal, Nabatchi, and De Graaf 2015)." The growing literature on public values in the last decade has moved from more philosophical discussions of the public interest to aspects of "publicness" (Bozeman 2007; Moulton 2009) or public values (e.g., Van Wart 1998; Rutgers 2019). Within public administration, public values have been at the forefront of many recent debates in different shapes and forms. Yet the literature is broad: Both the concept and content of public values differ widely among scholars (Beck Jørgensen and Bozeman 2007; Bozeman 2007). One complicating matter is, for example, that many authors do not explicitly distinguish between *public values* and *public value* (singular), focusing on the managerial approaches and strategies aimed at value creation that move beyond New Public Management (Moore 1995, 2013; De Graaf and Van der Wal 2017). Both concepts are only in some ways related and concern different debates and approaches in public management (Bozeman 2002; Bryson, Crosby, and Bloomberg 2014; Van der Wal, Nabatchi, and De Graaf 2015). Generally speaking, the public *value* approach is about the desired outcomes of governance. It "is an approach that asserts a need for public managers to realize the public values of their policy activities. This is the 'public good' and collective benefit of public policy" (Haynes 2018: 981). The public *values* approach concerns those principles, conditions, and qualities of processes, persons, and institutions that enable (public) actors to pursue and achieve public value.

Yet even when we focus on *public values*, "Scholars are drawn to many different aspects of public values, resulting in a fragmented literature serving varied purposes" (Bozeman and Johnson 2015: 2). The concept of public values has been used in many different ways. It can refer to concrete goals such as the reliability and safety of public transport (De Bruijn and Dicke 2006; Weihe 2008; Steenhuisen 2009a), to procedural- and process-related aspects of governance such as accountability and transparency (Weihe 2008), and to moral concepts of right and wrong that guide or should guide public action (Van Der Wal 2008).

Addressing public values in general, some people propose sets of public values prima facie (Tait 1997; Gregory 1999); others derive sets of specific public values (e.g., equity or lawfulness) through empirical research (Beck Jørgensen 2006; Van der Wal, De Graaf, and Lasthuizen 2008). This does not help with classification. Transparency – to give one example – can be considered a procedural value, a concrete goal, *and* a moral value. And in public policy, public values as concrete goals, procedural values, and moral values always interact. The decision to achieve a certain goal is always preceded by an idea about what a good society entails and about the role public administration should play in the realization of this goal. And in between practical goals and moral ideas, stand procedures that represent and institutionalize the appreciation of certain values related to processes. Consequently, examples of *public* values mentioned in the literature vary widely. Nevertheless, their study must be pursued. Beck Jørgensen and Bozeman (2007: 355): "There is no more important topic in public administration and policy than public values ... if researchers can advance, even incrementally, the study of public values beyond its current ambiguous and unbounded status, then those advances could serve many different theory developments and even practical purposes."

1.5 Why the Values of Public Governance Should Be Studied

All meaning is normative (De Graaf, Hoenderboom, and Wagenaar 2010). As Putnam (2002: 30) claimed, values and normativity permeate all our experiences. When people interact, values play a role – value-free interaction does not exist (Van Steden, Van Putten, and Hoogland 2019: 280). This also applies to public governance: Values are inseparable from the public realm (Beck Jørgensen and Bozeman 2007; Meijer and De Jong 2020). There is no such thing as a neutral state, nor is there such a thing as a neutral public organization (Gawthrop 1998). Appraisal – valuing – is an essential part of public administration (Self 1982). Rutgers (2015: 6): "This may range from weighing the visual impact of a new building on a skyline to evaluating the risks of a terrorist attack. The criteria for judging relevance and meaning in all such assessments are primarily public values: Is it legal, efficient, democratic, is it a public concern to begin with?" Somehow we have to deal with the very normativity of public governance (Rutgers 2015). Ringeling (2017: 34): "A Public Administration that refrains from studying these value problems is a lame duck … In the analysis of the values in doctrines of Public Administration, discussions about values should be at the heart of the discipline."

The impact of the non-neutral state in Western countries on personal, social, societal, and cultural values and on the lives of its citizens is enormous. "One of the most striking features of the welfare state is its extraordinary growth over the course of the twentieth century" (Heath 2020: 176). The German economist Adolph Wagner came up with a law named after him, which states that state spending increases as the national income increases. Or simply put: The richer the country, the bigger the state, irrespective of the ideological background of the government. Even conservative government leaders such as Margaret Thatcher and Ronald Reagan made tax systems less egalitarian but yet expanded total public spending. Heath (2020) supports a simple and convincing reason for this being the case. As citizens get richer, they want to spend a larger portion of their income on public goods. Once basic needs are provided for, there is a demand for sanitation, security, or healthcare, all goods best provided by public governance. Welfare states tax the population heavily to be able to carry out extensive health programs, adopt pension policies, and provide an education system.

Since all of these public programs, policies, and actions by public institutions have an enormous impact on society and on every citizen's life (Putters 2021), it is important to study them. Where are the important decisions about public policies made? The answer is: Everywhere in public governance. Often public governance is described as elected politicians engaging in normative considerations and deciding about the values and ends, with administrators exerting technical discretion to find the best means to attain them (Zacka 2022: 24). Zacka (2022) provides convincing reasons that this picture is not accurate: It understates the extent to which administrative agencies participate in policy making, and the extent to which bureaucrats have to make value judgements when implementing policies.

In his seminal *When the State Meets the Street*, Zacka (2017) describes the implicit but coherent moral structure of the commonplace decision-making of street-level bureaucrats – "too often dismissed as soulless operators." Public policies are characterized by much discretionary and autonomous power. Heath (2020: 17): "Even the NPM reforms, which were largely motivated by the desire to *curb* bureaucratic entrenchment and budget maximization, wound up dramatically increasing the autonomy of civil servants." Public organizations and public officials cannot be neutral actors. They play an important role in the allocation of values; policies can be interpreted in different ways, public organizations have the discretion to promote certain values over others, and they are not only involved in the implementation of policy, but also in the formulation of policies (Ringeling 2017).

1.6 The Importance of Studying the Values and Value Conflicts in Modern-Day Governance

So, studying the values of public governance has always been important, but it is now of more importance than ever. Nowadays, public governance is living in a new and still relatively untested age. We see greater fragmentation in social and political life. Public governance is more and more differentiated (Bevir 2010), and public administration continues to evolve into new forms of public governance (Sørensen and Torfing 2018). These developments have gone hand in hand with other massive social, political, economic, and technological changes: individualization, globalization, information technology, and many more (Boutellier 2011). As a result, institutions disaggregate and realign in increasingly complex forms; hybridization and collaboration are becoming increasingly the norm, while more formal institutional arrangements wither. Next to the traditional state actors, all kinds of other actors – such as citizens (including angry citizens), companies, and societal partners – play an ever-larger role in public governance.

Important developments in Western governance, according to Rhodes (2007), include the move from government to governance with shifting boundaries between the state and civil society. He speaks of "hollowing out the state," a new "differentiated polity" and developments toward "network governance" (Rhodes 2007: 1248), implying that the traditional instruments of government co-mingle, compete, and conflict with the new instruments of governance to variable effects (Rhodes 2007: 1253). The institutions and principles shaping the behavior and decisions of public actors change and become more diffuse. Torfing et al. (2012: 1): "One major change has been the increasing complexity of policy problems, and the increasing interdependency of policy areas, policy levels, and policy actors. Making appropriate public policy has never been easy, but is has become all the more difficult." Because of developments such as outsourcing, privatization, public–private partnerships (PPP), and DBFMO (Reynaers and De Graaf 2014), a significant number of public goods and services – roads, public transport, education, healthcare – are now produced or delivered by or in close collaboration with private partners. Furthermore, Fischer (2005) speaks of *participatory* governance; the increasing role of citizens – often called public/citizen *participation* – in public governance has been widely acknowledged (Nabatchi and Leighninger 2015). Ansell and Gash (2007) speak of *collaborative* governance to describe how public and private stakeholders together in collective agencies engage in consensus-oriented decision making. Bovaird (2007) writes about "a radical reinterpretation of the role of policy making and service delivery in the public domain" and calls for studies on (community) *coproduction* (Brandsen and Honingh 2015; Voorberg, Bekkers, and Tummers 2015), or *co-creation* (Brandsen, Steen, and Verschuere 2018). Ansell and Torfing (2018) describe *interactive* governance as the interaction between a plethora of public and private actors as the vehicle for initiating, designing, and implementing policies and regulations.

These developments in public governance lead to new dilemmas for all (public) actors in different forms (Rhodes 2007: 1254). If the traditional institutions are less influential, this has consequences for values and *value conflicts*. Inevitably, the new arrangements (Koppenjan and Klijn 2004; Osborne 2006) have a direct influence on the ethics of governance and on value conflicts (Macaulay 2018: 286). The concept of public values remains at the heart of each of these many manifestations of governance (Bryson, Crosby, and Bloomberg 2014). As new forms have emerged, we have witnessed a parallel rise in the ways we try to understand integrity and ethics. Bevir (2012: 12): "The word 'government' characteristically sits best with a moral or empirical belief in a homogenous nation under a unified state. The word 'governance' evokes more plural moral and empirical visions." New governance arrangements lead to *changing* and *new* public value conflicts (De Graaf and Meijer 2013) – where such values as transparency, participation, or accessibility are suddenly at odds with efficiency, stability, or democratic processes (e.g., Sørensen 2002; Sørensen and Torfing 2005; Sørensen and Torfing 2009). Involving private partners in public governance means posing problems with the values of transparency and legitimacy, as private partners are not democratically elected (Bevir 2010; Reynaers and De Graaf 2014). With diffuse responsibilities and accountabilities, public administrators find it hard to safeguard traditional public values such as equality, democracy, and transparency (Bevir 2012: 12; Nederhand et al. 2018).

Concrete examples of value conflict in new governance arrangements include policies coping with climate change; governments increasingly involve citizens and (semi-)private stakeholders in formulating and executing adaptation policies (Bovaird et al. 2015; Ianniello et al. 2019). Private parties are involved in decisions about a "fair" distribution of the costs and subsidies. However, participation and accessibility are at odds with efficiency, stability, and traditional democratic processes (Sørensen 2002; Sørensen and Torfing 2005; Rijksoverheid 2018).

When we look at the literature on new governance arrangements, concerns about specific public values crop up. About half of American public administrators believe that the blurring of boundaries between the private and the public sector has had the effect of subjugating civic values to commercial value (Bowman and Knox 2008). As we saw in the area of public care, equality is often mentioned as a value under threat: "One possible implication concerns distribution: the potential advantages of coproduction for citizens and governments notwithstanding, scholars have found that participants in coproduction come primarily from wealthy communities. Thus, the apprehension arises that coproduction can perpetuate and worsen the disproportionate control over community resources possessed by the more affluent" (Clark, Brudney, and Jang 2013: 690).

Another example comes from Bevir (2010: 270), who points out that participatory governance can lead to less formal equality. Decision-making processes change in the sense that different people participate. "The rules and manner of participating and reaching decisions may vary in large part with those who are actually involved. Legitimacy is thus less likely to derive from a kind of formal equality than from principles such as openness of the process, the participation of relevant individuals, and the perceived fit between the process and the situation it is meant to address" (Bevir 2010: 270).

In the Netherlands, in public care ("Wet Maatschappelijke Ondersteuning"), where citizen participation and responsibilities have both increased, public consultants and citizens discuss together in "kitchen table" conversations who will get access to what in order to deliver customized services. But there are grave concerns that this leads to arbitrariness and ineffective care, and there are doubts about whether the public administrator will find delivering a customized service compatible with working efficiently and lawfully (Meurs 2018).

Several private stakeholders are actively involved in the matter of sheltering refugees. In the city of Nijmegen, for example, local residents in the neighborhood around an emergency reception center developed horizontal relations within and beyond the walls of the center, using social media platforms (Smets et al. 2017). They organized different types of activities, and this led to tension with the shelter authorities. Many of the activities they arranged were disapproved of because they did not comply with safety regulations, or because they did not treat all 3,000 refugees equally and might cause envy (Smets et al. 2017). During *Sinterklaas* festivities, children were only allowed to receive presents if they all got the *same*, small, safe toy.

Political loyalty and professionalism are among the other values mentioned as being currently under threat: "While some public values such as responsiveness and innovation might be fostered in co-production, others such as political loyalty or professionalism might be threatened. Balancing these values is already difficult within the public sector, but it is even more challenging in multi-actor settings where professionals and citizens sometimes promote incommensurable values. Research on conflicting values in collaborative settings is scarce" (Aschhoff and Rick 2018: 775–76).

A frequently mentioned area of conflict is between democratic participation on the one hand and transparency and accountability on the other: "Governance through the formation of networks composed of public and private actors might help solve wicked problems and enhance democratic participation in public policy making, but it may also create conflicts and deadlocks and make public governance less transparent and accountable" (Sørensen and Torfing 2009: 234).

Bovaird specifically mentions accountability as a public value that is under threat. His strongest concern about coproduction – blurring the boundaries between the public, private, and voluntary sectors – is that it may dilute public accountability (Bovaird 2007: 856).

Interestingly, some authors question the moral value of participation and are afraid that when valued too highly, this may lead to ineffectiveness and inefficiency: "Not only are co-creation and co-production seen as instrumental tools for enhancing the quality and democratic quality of public service delivery, they are often regarded as a virtue in themselves. This implies that even if outcomes such as increased efficiency or effectiveness of public services are lacking or remain unproven, co-creation and co-production are still seen as holding a positive value in themselves (cf. Voorberg, Bekkers, and Tummers 2015: 1346). This is dangerous" (Steen, Brandsen, and Verschuere 2018: 7).

As has become clear in this section, there are concerns about the values of efficiency, effectiveness, stability, democracy (democratic participation), equality, uniformity, professionalism, transparency, and accountability in new governance arrangements. Yet, the evidence of which public values conflict under what conditions remains scarce. So, too, does the extent to which public administrators are genuinely faced with making choices among conflicting values. Wagenaar (1999: 444) claims that "public programs are structured in such a way that they regularly confront the administrator with difficult value choices." According to Spicer (2001), there is good reason to assert that value conflicts are especially pervasive in public administration, where statutes and regulations that seek to reconcile multiple values in practice often present administrators with conflicting signals. A VBG perspective in the discipline of Public Administration can answer questions like: Which values are important in Western public governance and which values conflict?

1.7 The Marginal Attention Paid to Values in the Discipline of Public Administration

Ringeling: "Values, it turned out, seem to be inevitable phenomena in the public sphere. Public administration had to deal with it. The same is true for the discipline that studies it" (Ringeling 2017). Yet, this is not the case, for the most part. Although public governance is value-laden, the normativity of governance has seldom taken center stage in the study of Public Administration (De Graaf 1996). Despite their omnipresence, values are under-acknowledged in studying public governance, "they are 'leached out' of positive policy analysis in favour of interest-based and institutionalist approaches" (Stewart 2009: 15). The same goes for Policy Studies and Political Science, Stewart (2009: 31):

> ... there is a deep structure of policy that the values perspective gets at, which other approaches do not. The reason we remain so distrustful of values is that the legacy of neo-Marxist structural analysis lives on, in the sense that political science always looks for interests, because interests are pre-eminently economic. And the primacy of the economic engine is always with us. As political scientists, we are trained to see values as epi-phenomena, lodged somewhere between interests and ideologies. If, at a seminar, you argue that something happened because it is in someone's interests for it to happen, there is always agreement. To argue that espoused values might also be real is to risk being labelled naïve. In this way, an easy cynicism is substituted for explanation.

The origins of Public Administration lie in a practical imperative: The search for solutions to (public) organizational problems where the dominant value was efficiency (Ringeling 2017: 44–45). Much of the discipline has always had the self-image of an instrumental discipline. Apolitically and neutrally advising the powers that be. Instrumental, not normative. The discipline of Public

Administration is mostly focused on professionalizing public governance (Braun et al. 2015), with the values of effectiveness and efficiency central.

This is not to say that the discipline of Public Administration has completely ignored (public) values. Some attention has certainly been paid. Just after World War II, Dahl (1947) pointed to three problems in the science of Public Administration. The first – and most important one – is that values and normativity are treated as somehow external to public administration, when clearly they are not. Dahl: "Writers on public administration often assume that they are snugly insulated from the storms of clashing values; usually, however, they are most concerned with ends at the very moment that they profess to be least concerned with them" (Dahl 1947: 2). Dahl makes a plea that the place of normative values be made clear.

In the seventies, some authors pointed to the value-laden practice of public administration. For example, Rein (1976: 140): "Above all, social policy is concerned with choices among competing values." And Fischer (1980: xiv): "Most of or social crises involve more than matters of inefficient programs, first and foremost, they involve basic value conflicts." A prominent example from the 1980s is Waldo's *Administrative State* (Waldo 1984), where a great deal of attention is paid to values in public administration.

The 1980s saw the rise of the "New Public Management" (NPM) and its associated doctrines of public accountability and organizational best practice (Hood 1995). NPM is often blamed for the current focus on effectiveness and efficiency and for driving all other values out of Public Administration theory (and practice, see Section 5). NPM has often been declared dead (e.g., Dunleavy et al. 2006), and one often reads that NPM has never been popular in the discipline of Public Administration. Whether or not that is true – and that partly depends on precisely how you define it – rationalization processes and the management perspective are as prominent as ever in both the discipline and the practice (see Section 5) of public governance; a technocratic management perspective is dominant in the discipline of Public Administration. According to Ringeling, the study of public administration "has become more and more comparable to what business administration does for the private sector: a study focused on optimizing government processes without reference to the political context and public values at stake ... Public administration is in my view a culture science with a normative character" (Ringeling 2017: 14–15). As Gawthrop (1998: 87) states, it is the logic of utility that still provides the basic rationale for the classical management tenets of efficiency and control. The concept of *public management* has taken center stage in the field of public administration. In this perspective, the values of doing well – effectiveness and efficiency – are central. This is at the expense of other values, and of attention, in general, to values.

In the last two decades, attention to *public values* has grown substantially (Bozeman 2007; Stewart 2009; Moore 2013; Van der Wal, Nabatchi, and De Graaf 2015; Van der Wal 2016). Yet, as discussed earlier, this is due to a heterogeneous group of authors (Rutgers 2015: 2), and the concept of public values has not succeeded in providing a well-defined focus for theory or praxis (Rutgers 2015: 2). The scholarly attention to values remains on the edges of the dominant public administration theories. Instead – according to Thacher and Rein (2004: 457) – a large proportion of current academic publications about public policy and management look for the most efficient ways to given ends (Lynn, Heinrich, and Hill 2000; Thacher and Rein 2004: 457). This instrumental rationality "has made many useful contributions to the understanding of improvement of policy decisions, but its contributions run out when policy does not pursue a single and overriding end . . . When a policy actor encounters a new situation in which its goals conflict, it may find that its preferences are simply unfinished. Existing models of policy rationality have great difficulty accommodating such situations" (Thacher and Rein 2004: 457–58). Following Herbert Simon (1957: 61), who stated "an administrative decision is . . . correct if it selects appropriate means to reach designated ends," many scholars evaluate administrative actions and policies in terms of their contribution to some coherent set of measurable goals (Spicer 2005: 541).

Sandel (1996) has argued that ignoring value dimensions does not mean a neutral state. "Time and again, the efforts to refrain from value judgments have resulted in value judgments" (Ringeling 2017: 53). Raz (2005) shows how instrumental rationality also has a normative character. Gawthrop criticizes the emphasis on rational objectivity in governance studies that leads to little tolerance for the expression of ethical-moral values:

> The evidence is mounting that the current cadres of public-sector careerists are, to put it charitably, immature in their comprehension of the ethical-moral democratic values . . . Indeed, professional schools have become very competent in training their students about what they *can* do . . . they are woefully inadequate in their efforts to prepare these same students to decide what they *should* do when faced with the distorted dynamics of work ethic whose role models are 'reinvented' clones of the Machiavellian school of management. (Gawthrop 1998: 19)

So, despite their importance in public governance, little attention is paid in the discipline of Public Administration to values and the conflict of values (Van der Wal, De Graaf, and Lawton 2011). A VBG perspective takes *value* as the central concept and thus enriches the field of PA: both, as argued so far, because of the account it gives of the important normative core of public governance, and the important explanatory possibilities it offers, as explained in the next section.

1.8 The Explanatory Possibilities of the VBG Perspective: Values Trump Interest

Even though it is more than a half century since Easton (1965) wrote the influential words that public policies are the means through which politics "allocates values," as we saw in the previous section most accounts of public governance give little prominence to the role of values: "values are either subsumed within accounts that stress the role of interests, institutions, and ideas (ideologies), or, within the broader context of political science, are conceived as convenient 'covers' for the pursuit of self-interest" (Stewart 2006: 183). "The reasons are not far to seek. Values are tricky to capture, changeable and much less robust than the more familiar forces of self-interest" (Stewart 2009: 1)

In the study of public governance, frequent use is made of network theories where the central concept is (conflicting) interests (in the case of Koppenjan and Klijn (2004): perceptions thereof). Public governance is seen as consisting of a multitude of persons and institutions with particular interests. Through constant negotiations between these interdependent parties – stakeholders – public governance takes shape (Bevir 2010).

Yet, next to interests, values can be the driving force behind the actions of individuals and institutions in public governance. As Arjo Klamer, a former alderman in the city of Hilversum, claims: "My civil servants are value driven. They operate on the basis of values, on what they find really important" (De Graaf 2016: 7). Stewart: "One of the main problems, I found, was the schizophrenic character of policy studies: the split between policy analysis as a form of normative social action and policy analysis as a mode of positivist explanation. From the point of view of those who 'do' policy, public policy is about values" (Stewart 2009: 7). Stewart (2009: 13) continues: "value positions are often linked to interests, but to describe them as ideologies puts the cart before the horse. An ideology is a value with hardening of the arteries. Interests can never be separated from values – both motivate our political activity." This is not to say that organizations and policies do not operate based on interests. "Interests can (and do) push and pull governments in different directions, but once a decision is made – the dam is built, the road goes through, the troops are dispatched to war – a choice between values has also been made" (Stewart 2009: 2). According to Haynes (2018: 992), we can think of values as important building blocks of complex policy systems.

Values are different from interests in an analytical sense. Because values are qualities that people find good – and because they are closely related to identities of individuals and groups (Rutgers 2011: 19) – it is very hard to negotiate over them, and compromise on them; much harder than compromising on interests. If you are convinced that human life is sacred and starts right after conception, it is hard to compromise on abortion issues (Stewart 2009). As Stewart (2009: 15) puts it succinctly: "Values trump interests." And she continues:

> Policy itself, whether it is public or not, performs a function which is quite clearly values-based. To construct a policy about anything is to try to make sense of the world. 'Every citizen over the age of 65 is eligible to receive an age-pension' may appear to be purely administrative policy, but it is one of many that constitute the values web of the welfare state, which promotes some version of social equity (Stewart 2009: 15).

There are many areas of public governance that are under-analyzed because the role of interests is actually less significant than assumed, and the role of value is much more significant. There is a deep structure of public governance that the VBG perspective gets at that other approaches do not (Stewart 2009). In the VBG perspective, values take center stage as the guiding concept in the theory and practice of public administration (Rutgers 2015; Fukumoto and Bozeman 2019) and are used as a *heuristic* to understand and analyze public governance (Stewart 2009: 4). The VBG perspective is not so much a theory or framework that can be "tested," it is used as a tool to understand and analyze public governance. One of the central concepts is not interests (stakes) held by stakeholders, but values held by valueholders.

Two key functions of values in public governance are identifiable: they are (1) motivators and (2) the basis for choice (Stewart 2009: 23). As said, values are closely connected to the identity of individuals and groups (Rutgers 2011: 19). As *motivators*, values help us to navigate our way through the world; they tell us what is good and bad. Rokeach (1979: 21), arguably the most cited axiologist: "Values operate as constituents of dynamics systems of social action because of their interconnectedness, their informational or directive effects, and their capacities to serve as 'carriers' of psychological energy."

Values tell us what is good and what is not. For a long time, it was assumed that in elections, citizens vote in their own interests. According to the Moral Foundation Theory (Haidt 2012), however, people vote according to their *moral* interests, in other words, their *values*. Political scientists have discovered that self-interest is a remarkably bad criterion for predicting political attitudes (Haidt 2012). The same goes for actors in public governance: The attitudes of governance actors are deeply structured by values (Haidt 2012). Political parties and interest groups strive to make their worries and interests become actual triggers of our moral modules.

Public governance – both the formulation of policies and the implementation thereof – are ripe with value *choices*.

> This is not to argue that powerful interests do not shape outcomes, or that electoral considerations do not frequently hold sway over policymakers. These factors are clearly highly significant. But once the choice is made (for example, the nuclear plant is put where it will be least politically damaging, rather than most environmentally safe), a polity has traded one value (safety) for another (political expediency) (Stewart 2009: 25).

Values choices are made about means as well as ends. Ringeling (2017: 235) speaks of a distinction between substantive and procedural values. Substantive values relate to "the good life." Procedural values refer to the standards according to which processes in the public sphere operate. The distinction is reminiscent to him of the distinction between "good" and "right." Procedural values, Ringeling maintains, can hardly be overestimated, yet he also stresses that procedural and substantive values are interrelated. Democracy and transparency, for example, are both procedural and substantive values. Throughout governance, choices about substantive and procedural values are made.

In public governance, values often come in webs or networks (Bryson, George, and Seo 2024). Public enterprises – such as policies – are imbued with an interconnected set of (procedural and substantive) values. Molina (2015), for example, speaks of clustered value systems that can conflict. And Haynes (2018: 985) notes when discussing Beck Jørgensen and Bozeman (2007): "Patterns of which values influence 'where' and 'when' [are] linked to the situational context. Context can be a mix of policy and professional typologies (Molina 2015). The complex mix of which values influence over time means that values have a dynamic interaction with policy and public management (Beck Jørgensen and Rutgers 2015; Beck Jørgensen and Vrangbæk 2011)."

Once values take center stage in the study and practice of public governance, we see an incompatibility between the – inherently non-negotiable – identified values and the necessarily compromise-based nature of policies and action in governance (Stewart 2009: 29). Richardson (1997) sees the plethora of values in public governance as its defining characteristic. Because value conflicts can be very destabilizing, much of public governance is dedicated to managing these conflicts since it abhors this particular type of conflict. Because of the overwhelmingly important role that values play in public governance, of necessity, strategies are deployed to reduce value conflict (more on this in Sections 4 and 5) (Stewart 2009).

Just as values and interests are closely linked, so are valueholders and stakeholders, certainly operationally. This is important to acknowledge in cases of cooperation and conflict resolution, as it is hard to negotiate over values and compromise on them; much harder than compromising on interests. "Interest however, are often amenable to compromise (Fisher and Ury 1981), while deep core beliefs tend to be nonnegotiable (Forester 2009; Haidt 2012; Sabatier and Weible 2007)" (Page et al. 2018: 241). This means that in public governance, it might sometimes be more fruitful to focus on interest after all and avoid a discussion of value. For more on this, see the collaboration literature, such as Page et al. (2018), Innes and Booher (2018), and Gray and Purdy (2018).

2 Theoretical Background of the Value-Based Governance Perspective

2.1 Epistemology: Language, Discourse, and Values

In the previous section, we have seen the need for a VBG perspective. It's time now to lay the theoretical groundwork of such a perspective. This section will discuss the epistemology of value research and will look at how values are made manifest. In particular, the importance of value pluralism for public governance will come under scrutiny. For empirical research that takes the VBG perspective, certain theoretical choices have to be made, and they are explained in this section.

Let's start with an epistemology for a VBG perspective. In past decades, discussions on the nature of "truth" have profoundly affected social research. Instead of assuming a given world "out there," waiting to be discovered, attention is being drawn to processes and ways through which the world is represented in language. The access we have to a reality outside language is highly problematic. Language does not simply report facts; it is not a simple medium for the transport of meaning. What is meant by – and the effect of – the words "She is corrupt" depends entirely on the context in which these words are spoken or written. Think, for example, about a judge speaking these words in the courtroom, as opposed to a man uttering them in a bar about the Danish queen. Du Gay (1996: 47): "The meaning that any object has at any given time is a contingent, historical achievement ... theorists of discourse argue that the meaning of objects is different from their mere existences, and that people never confront objects as mere existences, in a primal manner; rather these objects are always articulated within particular discursive contexts." Perhaps it *is* the case, as some philosophers claim, that what exists in the world necessarily exists (independent of human beings or language), but things can only be differentiated through language. The world itself does not give meaning to objects; this is done through language. In other words, although things might exist outside language, they get their meanings through language.

This view of language implies the possibility of describing public governance as a discursive construction. The meaning of anything always exists in particular discursive contexts; meaning is always contextual, contingent, and historical.

There have been many interpretations of discourse and discourse theory (Alvesson and Karreman 2000). In daily language, for example, a discourse can be defined as a conversation. But within the social sciences, the concept has a wider meaning. Here, a discourse is defined as "a specific ensemble of ideas, concepts and categorizations that are produced, reproduced and transformed in a particular set of practices and through which meaning is given to physical and social realities" (Hajer 1995: 44). For example, psychiatric discourse brought the idea of an unconscious into existence in the nineteenth century (cf. Foucault 1977; Phillips and Hardy 2002: 3). Discourses contain groups of statements that provide a way of talking and thinking about something, thereby giving meaning to social reality. Discourses are not "out there" between reality and language; they are not just a group of signs – they refer to practices that systematically form the objects we speak of. Discourse is not just a "way of seeing" – a worldview – but is embedded in social practices that reproduce the "way of seeing" as "truth." Discourses are constitutive of reality (De Graaf 2001). What is and is not true, the things we discuss – these cannot be seen outside discourse; they are internal to it. By looking at what people say and write, we can learn how their world is constructed. The concept of discourse is often used to overcome oppositions such as "action and structure" or "individual and structure." Since discourses, as used here, institutionalize the way of talking about something, they produce knowledge and thereby shape social practices. Social interactions cannot be understood without the discourses that give them meaning. Discourses function as a structure to behavior; they both enable and constrain it.

Like meaning, *values are immanent features of language*. Language is not a neutral means of communication: The use of language contains normative commitments. When we give meaning to something, we are also valuing it. Even though a Durkheimian view is clearly not endorsed here (with an emphasis here on language instead of institutions), there is a parallel. To Durkheim social institutions, collective ways of thinking, feeling, and doing are not empty but full of values (values give meaning to relationships). In a similar fashion, discursive practices are not empty; they are filled with values. By giving something a name, we highlight certain aspects. But in that same process, all other possible qualities are placed in the background or even ignored. Values, causal assumptions, and problem perceptions affect each other. In our daily lives, we so often jump between normative and factual statements that we do not fully realize the extent to which the way we see facts determines whether we see problems in the first place. But when we study our discussions more carefully, we can see that the "is" and the "ought" are intertwined. Seemingly technical positions in discourses on corruption (for example, "was he bribed or not?") conceal normative commitments. Discourses make more than claims of reality – they accomplish what Schön and Rein (1994) have called the "normative leap" or the connection between a representation of reality and its consequences for action. Within most versions of discourse theory, the strict dichotomy between facts and values ceases to make sense. Facts and values here are not treated as ontologically different; discourse theory treats them as different sides of the same coin. The "is" and "ought" shape each other in countless ways. Language is thus neither neutral nor static in communicating meaning. The awareness that language does not neutrally describe the world is important for public administration. Subtle linguistic forms and associated symbolic actions shape our convictions and presuppositions (Twist 1994: 79).

The theory that all meaning is normative is very influential nowadays among philosophers (Rutgers 2011: 14). Public governance is a linguistic, social, and normative construction: We can talk meaningfully about policies, which is something quite different from politics (Rutgers 2011: 5). Factual explanations and descriptions in governance are pervaded with values; it matters how a given fact is valued. Seemingly objective concepts such as "management" or "public servant" have many different meanings and provoke very different value judgments (Rutgers 2011: 5). Rutgers (2011: 16) asks: Is a statement like "This is a bureaucratic organization" a description or an evaluation? The fact-value distinction is purely analytical, which also explains the interest in framing in public governance that has been seen in recent decades (e.g., De Bruijn 2011).

2.2 Value Pluralism

Within the VBG perspective here, the theoretical stance of *value pluralism* is taken (cf. Hinman 2013), arguably most famously defined by Isaiah Berlin (1982: 69): "[T]here might exist ends – ends in themselves in terms of which alone everything else was justified – which were equally ultimate, but incompatible with one another, that there might exist no single universal overarching standard that would enable a man to choose rationally between them."

Values can be incompatible. Value incompatibility, simply put, means that pursuing certain values inevitably limits the ability to pursue certain other values (Spicer 2001: 509). The idea that values inherently conflict or are in some situations incompatible is hardly new; many social scientists have researched it (e.g., Brecht 1959). Isaiah Berlin (1992: 12) pointed out:

> What is clear is that values can clash ... They can be incompatible between cultures, or groups in the same culture, or between you and me. You believe in always telling the truth, no matter what; I do not, because I believe that it can sometimes be too painful and too destructive ... Both liberty and equality are among the primary goals pursued by human beings through many centuries; but the total liberty for wolves is death to the lambs, total liberty of the powerful, the gifted, is not compatible with the rights to a decent existence of the weak and the less gifted.

From the standpoint of value pluralism, however, values are not just often incompatible; they can also be incommensurable. The philosopher Elijah Millgram (1997) argued that commensurability – the consideration that each value identified as relevant to a choice can be recast in terms of its contribution to a single overarching value – is not plausible. Using wording very similar to Berlin (1982), Stephan Lukes (1989: 125) interprets incommensurability to mean that, "There is no single currency or scale on which conflicting values can be measured, and that where a conflict occurs no rationally compelling appeal can be made to some value that will resolve it. Neither is superior to the other, nor are they equal in value." This does not mean that agents cannot make choices or give reasons for them, "rather, it means that some of the reasons we might offer in support of making a particular choice are incommensurable with other reasons we might offer were we to make an alternative choice" (Spicer 2001: 512).

Famous examples of the incommensurable nature of important values in daily life are the conflict between money and friendship (Raz 1988; Lukes 1989; Spicer 2010). Sometimes we have to choose between spending time to make money and spending time with friends; how do we weigh that? We make such choices, yet we cannot pay for friendship, for then it would not be friendship. "Our ordinary experience of the incommensurability among our values denies the monistic claim made by a variety of ethical philosophers, whether deontological or utilitarian, that there is 'a common basis ... a single reason behind moral claims' (Hampshire 1983: 118)" (Spicer 2009: 539).

2.3 Value Pluralism in Public Governance

Many scholars in different fields such as philosophy and political theory have written about value pluralism, yet Spicer claims: "much of general public administration discourse has ignored the idea of value pluralism and has implicitly taken, as its premise, a monist or a unified conception of the good in which it is assumed that all values or goods can, at least in principle, be brought into harmony which each other" (Spicer 2001: 508). Yet, value pluralism is very relevant for public governance. According to Berlin (1992: 12), values conflict not only within individuals, but also between cultures and culture groups, or "between you and me." "This multifaceted character of value conflict is important, because it means that value conflicts present individuals or institutions with not simply a moral problem, but also a political problem" (Spicer 2001: 510). And more importantly, Spicer: "value pluralism would seem especially relevant to the experience of public administration where practitioners are often called upon to grapple with and make judgments about value conflicts, when making policy decisions, and where their actions are often, either explicitly or implicitly, coercive in character and affect a large number of people" (Spicer 2009: 539). The pursuit of an important value in governance inevitably limits the pursuit of other values. For example, Okun (1975) showed in his classic work that equality and efficiency necessarily conflict with each other in public policies.

Many ethnographic studies of particular administrators and public professionals (e.g., Skolnick 1967; Lipsky 1980; Maynard-Moody and Musheno 2003; Zacka 2017) show that public actors actually do not treat values as commensurable in daily public governance practice; intrinsically desirable public values conflict so choices have to be made (De Graaf and Van der Wal 2010; Van der Wal, De Graaf, and Lawton 2011). "Public administrators are often faced with making difficult choices or judgments among incompatible and incommensurable values" (Spicer 2009: 541). On a daily basis, the decisions in the public administration context involve contending with multiple, diverse, and often conflicting values (O'Kelly and Dubnick 2005: 394). "Irresolvable value conflict, a condition that in moral philosophy is called value pluralism, is intrinsic to contemporary political and administrative life" (Wagenaar 1999: 441). In public governance, there are many "conflicts that not even an all knowing and resource-unlimited God could resolve without wrongdoing" (Talisse 2015: 8). This is precisely what administrators experience. Thacher and Rein:

> Based on an examination of practice in crime policy, retirement policy, and refugee policy, we argue that policy actors often do not treat conflicting values as commensurable. Instead, they cope with value conflict by drawing from a repertoire of alternative strategies . . . As we explain throughout, none of these three strategies requires commensurability among values, but each can be a rational response to conflicting public values (Thacher and Rein 2004: 458).

Being a value monist entails maintaining that any conflict between things of value is necessarily subject to a unique and singular resolution. Any account of value monism in public governance should incorporate an idea of *which* value or good is the only intrinsic value or good to be upheld in public governance. Even though they are scarce, there are a few explicit value-monist accounts in the public administration literature. For example, some scholars judge the goodness of governance (see also Section 5) by one overriding value or norm, such as impartiality (Rothstein and Teorell 2008). Rothstein and Teorell (2008) mention competing conceptions such as democracy, the Rule of Law, or effectiveness/efficiency. None of these accounts can claim many followers. Apparently, it is not easy to convince people that value monism applies in public administration. To recognize value conflicts in public governance means rejecting monism. In monism, there is always a right action, and regrets should not be possible. Yet we *do* have regrets and dilemmas. There is moral conflict on all levels. Berlin: "Antigone is faced with a dilemma to which Sophocles implies one solution, Sartre offers the opposite, while Hegel proposes 'sublimation' on some higher level – poor comfort to those who are agonized by dilemmas of this kind" (Berlin 1992: 13).

Scholars such as Wagenaar (1999) try to understand how *individuals* handle moral conflict. As interesting as that is, it does not reveal the nature of intrinsic value conflict in public governance, which is the central focus here for a VBG perspective. Intrinsic value conflicts take many forms and exist at different levels: individual (public actors), governmental (formal institutions), and policy formation (allocation of values). Spicer:

> In other words, value conflicts can make themselves known at personal, interpersonal, intergroup, and intercultural levels. This multifaceted character of value conflict is important to recognize, because it means that value conflict presents individuals or groups with not simply a moral problem in terms of what they ought to do. It also present them with a political problem in terms of how different individuals and groups, who happen to hold different and conflicting values, should live together (Spicer 2010: 20).

Value pluralism is an important part of the theoretical foundation of the VBG perspective. Using this perspective, the next section will focus mainly on establishing empirically *which* values conflict in public governance, while Section 4 will outline the *strategies* used to deal with these conflicts.

2.4 Dilemmas: "we are doomed to choose"

The existence of value pluralism entails conflicting values and dilemmas at all levels of public governance. Since these conflicts and dilemmas play an important role in the VBG perspective, the concept and occurrence of dilemmas in public governance deserve further exploration.

The word dilemma comes from Greek: di-lemma, meaning two lemmas (fundamental propositions). The clashing of values is a necessary condition for a dilemma to arise. That means that every dilemma has a moral dimension. After all, values are at stake. That makes every dilemma a *moral* dilemma. Note that morality is then not seen as a practice that is distinct and separate from all others; moral reasoning is here not identified as a separate special kind of reasoning (Dubbink 2008), which would be the Kantian position: "The opposition between a moral reason and any other kind of reason permeates the *Critique of Practical Reason* (1788). It is sometimes said that Aristotelean thinking downplays the stand-alone position of moral reasons" (Dubbink 2008: 696).

A dilemma is always in the eyes of the beholder. If two persons have different values, they will have different dilemmas. When a (moral) decision is taken and the actor experiences that routine procedures and rules fit the situation, there is no dilemma for them, no conflict. That also means that the decision will probably not be discussed with colleagues or at dinner with the spouse. There is no need for justification after all.

The clashing of values is a necessary, but not a sufficient condition for a dilemma to arise. A dilemma cannot – neither in governance nor in daily life – be routine. A dilemma involves conflict, and we do not experience that continuously. That does not mean that administrators do not take many moral decisions on a daily basis; many of them do (e.g., Maynard-Moody and Musheno 2003; Pesch 2005; Zacka 2017), but when standard rules and decisions are applied, it is not experienced as a dilemma. Many value conflicts are dealt with in rules and standard procedures. Also, a dilemma does not end when making a decision (Dubbink 2008). Perhaps a state of paralysis is avoided, but the value consequences are still there (see Section 4).

There are several values that are generally considered intrinsic to public governance. For example, Beck Jørgensen & Sørensen (2013: 85) show that the codes of good governance that have been developed in fourteen countries all contain a set of public values. When comparing the different codes, they conclude that there seems to be a list of universal public values mentioned in nearly every code: "It seems fair to conclude that we have identified a set of global values." Beck Jørgensen & Sørensen conclude that there are nine public values – including transparency, impartiality, effectiveness, accountability, and legality – that are supposed to form the basis of all governmental actions. Few will dispute their importance in public governance. But there is no convincing argument that any one of these values is overriding and more important than the others. Pursuing these values in daily public governance reveals that not all of them can be upheld at the same time; some will be achieved at the expense of others. And since they are *intrinsic*, that means a moral wrong is committed. As Talisse (2015) correctly states: Value pluralists believe public governance is by necessity morally flawed, and this is also acknowledged by the many who write about dirty hands (e.g., Nieuwenburg 2014).

Dilemmas are an integral part of the public policy level, "all public policies hold important values in tension, either directly, through compromises and trade-offs, or indirectly, by excluding or marginalizing other approaches" (Stewart 2009: 186). Several scholars have argued this point and provided ample examples. Bailey (1964: 237), for example, argued half a century ago:

> The bittersweet character of all public policy needs little further elaboration: welfare policies may mitigate hunger but promote parasitic dependence; vacationing in forests open for public recreation may destroy fish, wild life, and through carelessness in the handling of fire, the forests themselves. Unilateral international action may achieve immediate results at the cost of weakening international instruments of conflict resolution. Half a loaf *may* be worse than no loaf at all. It also may be better in the long run but worse in the short run – and vice versa.

At the individual level there is, according to Spicer, "very good reason to believe that, in fact, value conflicts pervade much of the experience of those who work in government and public administration" (Spicer 2010: 31). According to Wagenaar "straight into their most minute technical rulings, ... the upshot is that administrators in the course of their everyday work, face thousands of large and small moral choices." Spicer again:

> This problem of choosing between morally disagreeable actions is often associated, especially nowadays, with extreme cases such as whether or not we ought to torture terrorists in order to obtain valuable information that could somehow save hundreds or thousands of lives. However the problem also exists in the seemingly more mundane activities of public administrators; as Udo Pesch (2005: 165) has pointed out that: 'the daily practice of the administrator appears to be overflowing with situations that give rise to the problem of ... dirty hands.' These dilemmas are often faced, for example, by street-level public administrators, such as social workers, in their ordinary day-to-day dealings with citizens, where, as Steven Maynard-Moody and Michael Musheno have vividly documented, 'the needs of individual citizen-clients exist in tension with the demands and limitations of rules' (2003: 93). (Spicer 2010: 33).

It can also be learned from Lipsky's seminal (1980) study or, later, the work by Maynard-Moody and Musheno (2003) that value conflict is unavoidable in public governance, it is a fact of administrative life. Decisions in public governance involve contending with diverse and often conflicting values (O'Kelly and Dubnick 2005: 394). "Public administrators are often faced with making difficult choices or judgments among incompatible and incommensurable values" (Spicer 2009: 541). Wagenaar (1999: 444) argues, "public programs are structured in such a way that they regularly confront the administrator with difficult value choices."

In a nutshell, in trying to realize intrinsic values in public organizations, intrinsic values conflict at all levels and lead to *dilemmas*. Dilemmas are interesting because in studying dilemmas, one studies which values are important in a given context. In a dilemma, there is conflict between two values that are apparently important. Here, the focus is not on solving dilemmas or in building a normative theory. Here, the focus is on a description of the oft-neglected normative side of public administration, the values of and in public governance. And for that purpose, dilemmas are interesting, because in studying dilemmas, one studies which values are important in a given context (see Section 3). In a dilemma, there is conflict between two values that are apparently important in someone's eyes. If one of them was not, there would not be a dilemma. *It is a very important aspect of conducting empirical research on values in public governance that, through studying dilemmas, the values trail can be uncovered.* As Stewart (2009: 30–31) observes about the value perspective as a comparative methodology (e.g., on inter-country differences):

> When identifying values and using them heuristically, an interesting phenomenon occurs. Searching for common values obviously will not do, as it is precisely in the differences in their interpretation of values, such as social equality, that countries most obviously differ. But another approach is possible, and that is to use tensions within and between different values (trade-offs) as a way of exploring difference... The values-based approach directs our attention as analysts to points of conflict – to places where March and Olsen's 'logic of appropriateness' starts to break down (March and Olsen 2006).

2.5 Conflicts as a Felt Problem for Individuals: Public Actors and Institutions

Value conflicts in governance take many forms and exist at different levels: individual (public actors), governmental (institutions), policy formation (allocation of values), and policy execution. Here, the focus is on value conflicts that "become manifest as a felt problem for individuals" (Thacher and Rein 2004: 461), especially when they present a challenge for *justification* (2006). Boltanski and Thévenot stress the differences in rationalities that actors can have in a dispute. Justifications have to follow the rules of acceptability. Thacher and Rein (2004: 461):

> When only a single overriding goal has primary relevance for policy making, it is clear what kind of argument a policy actor needs to offer to justify her actions: she must show that the choice she made is the best way to achieve that single overriding goal. But when multiple and conflicting values are relevant, it is not clear what kind of argument is needed to vindicate her decision ... In addition, she will need to justify her choice to pay more attention to one value at the expense of the others, or offer an alternative reason for her decision.

So, in the tradition of philosophical ethics, much focus here – especially in the empirical research in the next two sections – will be on individuals (public actors). This does not at all mean that institutions do not matter, on the contrary. According to some philosophers (e.g., Thompson 1985), ethical opinions in public governance are a personal trait of the public actor. Here, a different, more institutional view is taken: institutions strongly affect the opinions and behavior of public actors. De Vries (2002: 310): "Organizational traits and the pressures posed by the environment of the organizations (i.e., community and city hall) are seen in these theories as the conditions that affect the behavior of the members of that organization. It is such pressures that determine the autonomy, which in terms of Selznick (1992, 1957), that [sic] permits public bureaucracies to preserve their distinctive values, competence, and roles." From the point of view of practical philosophy, institutions provide their inhabitants with "repertoires of practical reasoning ... a moral disposition is not merely a disposition to act but also to deliberate in certain ways" (Nieuwenburg 2004: 686). In other words, the public actor's justification of a decision in a dilemma over conflicting values is always within the conditions of possibility of what can and cannot be said in the discourses of the public actor's institution. Nevertheless, they are not seen here as *completely* shaped by institutions. O'Kelly and Dubnick (2005: 397): "We argue that the day-to-day running of these institutions requires an understanding that the public administrators who maintain institutions face dilemmas in the carrying out of their work." In the tradition of Giddens (1981), it is assumed here that structures shape people's actions, but also presuppose them (Sewell 1992). Institutional arrangements are not independent forces; they are shaped by the actions of public actors (Giddens 1981). Thus, governance is shaped by individuals who follow rules, but no rule is self-interpreting (Wittgenstein 2006) and no choice is governed unequivocally by a single rule (Boltanski and Thévenot 1999, 2006). So, although built on the insights of institutionalism, an essential role is preserved here for the public actor.

It is important to note that studies on institutions have revealed that rules and conventions of governance can help to protect or prevent public actors from experiencing value conflicts as a problem, minimizing the sharpness of conflicts (Lindblom 1959; Wildavsky 1983; Thacher and Rein 2004). Institutions can provide one unifying value, preventing conflicts, or mechanisms can be in place to transfer conflicting values into a decision (Shepsle 1979). For example, a policy actor in conflict can choose efficiency with the justification that it is the main responsibility of someone else to look after integrity. That does not mean, however, that all value conflicts can be avoided, Thacher and Rein: "Institutional design can rarely protect actors from experiencing value conflict and its associated justificatory challenges entirely. Value conflict is always a problem of practice" (Thacher and Rein 2004: 461). Bowman and Knox (2008) found that virtually every American administrator (97 percent) believes that all public actors encounter ethical dilemmas at work. And it was already noted that *all* policies contain value conflicts, whether the actors carrying out that policy experience that or not. Also, because public governance has many stakeholders, even when institutions prevent public actors from perceiving a dilemma, it is likely that the perception of other stakeholders and subsequent action (from (social) media, for example) will force the public actor to justify the decision. And, thus, value conflicts come to the surface. Value conflict can thus be used to overcome the identification problem – which entails knowing a public value when we see it – that Fukumoto and Bozeman (2019) address in public values research. As said, through studying dilemmas, the values trail can be uncovered.

2.6 The VBG Perspective

Now we have an epistemology of a VBG perspective, as well as an understanding of value pluralism and dilemmas. As was argued in the first section, policy processes are often – theoretically as much as descriptively – depicted as technocratic processes. In most accounts of public governance, values get little prominence and are "either subsumed within accounts that stress the role of interest, institutions, and ideas (or ideologies), or, within the broader context of political science, are conceived as convenient 'covers' for the pursuit of self-interest. Whereas values are all pervasive, the all-important value dimension is neglected" (Stewart 2006: 183).

The VBG perspective brings values to the fore: the study of values and value conflicts in public governance is central. For the study of Public Administration, this is important because public policies are the means through which politics "allocates values" (Easton 1965), so through the VBG perspective, an important dimension of public governance is studied empirically. This is very much needed because, according to Oldenhof, Wehrens, and Bal (2022: 2):

> Despite the 'turn to values' in the field of Public Administration (West and Davis 2011: 226), the majority of studies still focuses on philosophical and theoretical discussions of values ... This conceptual interest in values has not been equally matched by empirical research ... there is a need for empirical research that investigates how multiple stakeholders – for example, public professionals, policymakers, and citizens – in interaction deal with contested value questions on the ground.

The VBG perspective is a theoretical perspective for conducting more of such empirical research. The next two sections are all about this kind of empirical research of public governance.

3 Empirical Research from a VBG Perspective

3.1 Introduction

The central concepts of the VBG perspective were discussed in the first section, and the theoretical background in Section 2. The *nature* of value conflict in public governance has been described, and the stance of value pluralism adopted. It has also become clear that the conceptual interest in values that the literature reveals has not been matched by empirical research (Van der Wal 2016; Oldenhof, Wehrens, and Bal 2022: 2). Even though several anecdotal empirical examples from previous studies were instanced, there are few empirical studies that adopt some sort of value-based approach. As a result, the literature provides few clues as to which values dominate in Western governance and which value conflicts are prevalent. In what follows, we address this gap in the literature. The focus in this (and the next) section is on empirical research from a VBG perspective. We answer questions such as: Which values are predominant in Western public governance, which specific value conflicts (dilemmas) are present, and what strategies are used to deal with these conflicts (next section)?

3.2 Strategies for Studying Values Empirically

One of the reasons empirical value research is so limited may be to do with the concept of value itself. As stated earlier, values are notorious for being highly abstract, essentially contested, and hard to define. They are even harder to make operational and to measure in empirical research (Espedal et al. 2021). Having defined values as qualities means that you cannot point values out; they are neither here nor there. Stewart (2009: 15–16): "while values are clearly important, they are difficult to detect and almost impossible to measure ... So we have something of a conundrum – public policy in its enacted sense, allocates values. Yet at the same time, we find it difficult to give convincing labels to the values that are enacted, because we lack the tools, indeed the language, to conceptualize what is going on." And: "Administrative systems rarely express their values directly. Rather they are contained in conventions, structures that set expectations and govern behavior" (Stewart 2009: 130).

Studying values empirically in public governance may not be straightforward, but it is possible, and qualities can be measured. To begin with, we know that values, as qualities, never come just by themselves; they never appear unaccompanied. Rather, they are always attached to people, processes, and practices. It is important to avoid objectifying them. Given the epistemological stance of the previous section, we cannot maintain that values are part of a transcendental realm within or behind reality. If values are seen as stable qualities existing in reality, they are still, in a sense, objectified. This would be the case when someone argues that something has an a priori value. Values are attributed within a specific practice – which is always within the confines of a specific context. The quality is not already out there. Values are qualities-in-use. It is very well possible that different qualities are attributed to the same phenomenon. The expression "attributed within a specific practice" is used here, and not "attributed by someone," because values are not private. Just as a private language does not exist (as Wittgenstein has shown), private values do not exist.

This approach to values is in an interpretivist tradition. Within this tradition, inductive approaches and strategies are commonly used to look for meaning in the subjective experiences of individuals engaging in social interaction: approaches looking for general value patterns that take contextual dependence and subjective nuance, variability, and meanings into account.

In the recent literature, several concrete strategies can be found to measure values in line with this. Several of them can be found in the book *Researching Values* (Espedal et al. 2022). One of them is by Paanakker (2020), who researches values and value conflicts by studying craftsmanship practices. This strategy focuses on exploring actors' perceptions and accounts of what constitutes craftsmanship in their work. Craftsmanship is defined as "the application of concrete skills, knowledge, and practices, that, according to public officials, are needed to deliver good work in street-level public service delivery," for instance, in education, patient care in hospitals, or detention (Paanakker 2021: 223). This informal and experiential knowledge is embedded in concrete, everyday craftsmanship practices and offers a wealth of valuable data on how values are enacted and how values conflict in real-life practice (Paanakker 2019). Actors' own perceptions of craftsmanship reveal what they deem important in the work context, what practical problems they face on the work floor, and how well their notion of craftsmanship is facilitated by their organization. The insights on concrete individual and organizational practices can then be used to analytically deduce the values they describe. This offers an interesting method for comparing the manifestation and enactment of values among professionals, but also for comparing different public sector levels (such as public managers and policy makers). Through collective sense-making, it shows how values in the public domain are powerful indicators of public sector behaviours and processes, but also of organizational problems and conflicts between different roles and responsibilities in the organization. As such, studying craftsmanship practices specifically enables the uncovering of the values trail throughout organizational hierarchies (De Graaf and Paanakker 2022).

A similar yet different research was adopted by Oldenhof, Wehrens, and Bal (2022), who used a pragmatic approach to investigate policy experiments in healthcare, more particularly by focusing on conflicting values in policy experiments that join multiple stakeholders in the co-design, experimentation, implementation, and evaluation of innovative policy ideas in local settings. Through interviews, they tried to avoid bias by not establishing an a priori set of values. A strategy was used to explore how respondents value something in context. For example, they might be asked, "How do you value an experiment as a 'good' experiment in your regional network?" (Oldenhof, Wehrens, and Bal 2022: 9).

Another type of approach to studying values makes use of several techniques from the evaluation literature and the public strategic management literature, such as value chains, theories of action, strategy maps, and principles-focused evaluation.

Yet another approach – the one central here – is to study dilemmas in public governance. As was seen in the previous section, in trying to realize intrinsic values within public organizations, there will be intrinsic values conflicts that cause dilemmas. And these dilemmas are interesting because in studying specific dilemmas, one is studying the (conflicting) values that are important in that given context. In a dilemma, there is conflict between two values that are apparently equally important. If one of them were less important, there would be no dilemma. For our purposes, the interest is not in solving dilemmas, in stating what the morally right thing to do is: it is more important to describe what the dilemmas are. Through studying dilemmas, we can uncover the values trail.

3.3 Cross-Case Conclusions about Five Previous Case Studies

3.3.1 Five Empirical Case Studies

Some research has been conducted to answer the empirical questions about which values dominate, which values conflict, and which value profiles dominate in public governance. Here, a cross-case analysis of five case studies is presented. These case studies were all conducted between 2011 and 2020 and focused on revealing which dilemmas are most common. They were conducted in different public governance settings, specifically, including references to their publications:

(1) a municipality (De Graaf, Huberts, and Smulders 2016),
(2) a hospital (De Graaf, Huberts, and Smulders 2016),
(3) the police (De Graaf and Meijer 2019),
(4) top public administration (De Graaf and Paanakker 2015), and
(5) the academic teaching environment (De Graaf 2021).

In all of these studies, evidence was sought on the question of *which* values conflict are found in public governance, and, in three cases, which *value profiles* can be assigned to public actors. The findings of these case studies can be found in the mentioned publications.

3.3.2 The Most Common Value Conflicts in the Case Studies

As stated in the previous section, value conflicts in public governance take many forms and exist at different levels: individual (public actors), governmental (institutions), policy formation (allocation of values), and policy execution. The choice of a particular case study, and especially the choice of a particular policy actor, logically determined the frequency of value conflicts found at each level. In the case of academic teachers, the focus was on a specific profession, so most value conflicts found were on an individual level. We saw the same in the case of the police, although in that case study – due to the fact that police officers as well as other functionaries were interviewed – more evidence was found on value conflicts on institutional and policy levels. The case of the municipality and especially the case of the top public administrators produced many examples of values conflicts at the policy level.

A cross-case analysis of the case studies gives a first impression of *which* values conflict most in Western public governance; since the case studies were all in one country, obviously, further analysis is needed to compare the initial impressions of these five case studies with other evidence. More on this later.

Value conflicts in several of the case studies were framed employing three types of governance, each of which focuses on a particular aspect of good governance. First is the idea of *performing governance*, which is related to values such as effectiveness and efficiency. An emphasis on this aspect of good governance is in line with, for instance, ideas on New Public Management (Hood 1991). A second type of governance is called *proper governance*. Key values of this type are integrity, lawfulness, and equality. *Responsive governance* is the third type. Values related to this type are transparency, participation, legitimacy, and accountability. These are values that have become more important to Western democracies during the last decades, partly as a result of technological developments and partly because of a changing role for governments in societies (cf. van Kersbergen and van Waarden 2004; Rhodes 2007).

In the cross-case analysis, the following four value conflicts stand out, in descending order of frequency:

(1) Efficiency versus effectiveness
(2) Transparency versus effectiveness
(3) Lawfulness versus effectiveness
(4) Participation versus efficiency

The conflict between effectiveness and efficiency was the most frequent conflict in all five case studies; it is a conflict between two values of performance governance (cf. Van Wart and Berman 1999). Van Wart and Berman (1999) asserted that even though public governance's productivity values change over time, at the core is a tension between effectiveness and efficiency (Zavattaro et al. 2021: 1450). Bøgh Andersen et al. (2012: 723): "Once the budgeted resources are used up, the public service provider faces a serious dilemma of either skimping on services or not being able to keep within the budget."

The other three dilemmas are all between a procedural and a performance value: the values of transparency and participation (both relating to responsive governance) and lawfulness (proper governance) conflict with either effectiveness or efficiency (performance governance). Since dilemmas point to the values that really matter – they uncover the values trail – we can conclude that these five values are of particular importance in these five case studies.

The other value conflicts found seem to say something about the specific profession/context in which they were encountered. Thirty-five of the forty-one dilemmas divulged in the academic teachers' case study fall within three categories: quality versus efficiency, quality versus equity, and equality versus reasonableness. So, the conclusion is that quality and efficiency are important to academic teachers. Other important values in that particular case were equality and reasonableness. A tension between professional (academic) and economic (managerial) value systems has been described in previous research that was done mainly in the UK, Australia, and New Zealand (Winter and O'Donohue 2012). By contrast, in the current case study of a public university, it is mostly the old institutional *professional* values (quality of teaching, equality, and reasonableness) that prevail among the academic teachers. This is very much in line with survey research in Australia (Winter and O'Donohue 2012), where academics who were lecturers and professors expressed a strong response to statements indicative of professional values (Winter and O'Donohue 2012: 568). Yet the tension and conflict over efficiency (an economic value) are also very clear in the case study here. In times of cutbacks, the tension between the professional and economic value systems is clearly prevalent.

It is interesting that it is mainly in the case of the police that there is conflict between two *procedural* values – namely, lawfulness and transparency. In the context of the police, comparatively speaking, the value of lawfulness is important.

In the case of the hospital, the conflict between efficiency and accountability is particularly important, so the value of *accountability* is to note here.

3.4 Evidence of Conditions that Influence Value Conflict

3.4.1 Stage of the Policy Process

The cross-case analysis reveals that in certain policy phases, value conflict is more prevalent. Earlier research by Anne-Marie Reynaers (2014) has shown that the importance of values differs at different stages of the policy process. This means there are different value conflicts at different stages. There is much evidence in the cases examined here that supports that conclusion. For example, the degree of transparency required depends strongly on the phase a particular policy process is in. During fact-finding in the policy formulation phase, transparency is easier, and involving stakeholders and keeping citizens informed can enhance their commitment. Conversely, in policy execution and oversight, transparency is perceived to be less in conflict with effectiveness. Also, lawfulness conflicts particularly with effectiveness when it comes to policy formation, and with efficiency when policy execution is involved.

To aldermen, value conflicts reside mainly in those situations where the public interest is at stake. Aldermen often claim that they weigh their decisions on the basis of the common good: Does my decision first and foremost contribute to the interest of the majority of the municipality? This indicates that the value of responsiveness or service is regarded as one of the most important values in aldermen's performance. Consequently, decisions that affect some (group of) citizens negatively are experienced as a dilemma. These value conflicts of policy execution are what aldermen have in common with street-level bureaucrats who experience similar dilemmas (Lipsky 1980; Maynard-Moody and Musheno 2003). Top administrators are much further away (physically and emotionally) from those who are affected by the policies they work on. Typical quotes from aldermen include: "I experience difficulty in decisions in which the interests of individual citizens are at stake" and "It is hard when you know a decision will hurt someone." One alderman gave the example of the construction of a road that would greatly benefit the accessibility of the private industry located at the borders of a village, but would seriously hamper the mobility of the village inhabitants, placing them in an infrastructural isolation. Here, the incommensurable nature of the values entailed in specific policies/goals becomes apparent.

3.4.2 Governance Context

The cross-case analysis also underlines something that was already assumed in Section 2: when it comes to value conflicts in public governance, the context is highly relevant. For example, compared to the municipality, respondents from the hospitals mentioned fewer value conflicts. This might have to do with the semi-public character of the hospital. Acting in a proper manner and being responsive to society are expected from both a municipality and a hospital, but are of less importance in the daily work of the latter. Most of the value conflicts that occur entail a conflict in which the effectiveness or efficiency of the treatment of individual patients is at stake.

3.4.3 Influence of Social Media

The nature of the value conflicts in public governance is constantly evolving and changing. The case study of the police clearly showed the influence of social media on public governance. The literature on (social) media highlights that these media are not value-neutral but contain a script that puts an emphasis on certain patterns of usage. The script emphasizes openness, engagement, and user-centrality, and the expectation is that this emphasis will result in a shift in the value conflicts that public officials are facing. Openness results in new conflicts around the value of transparency, engagement triggers new conflicts around participation, and user-centrality triggers more conflicts around equality.

3.4.4 Politicians Versus Administrators

The comparison of "Governing good versus governing bad" revealed – not unexpectedly – that politicians face value conflicts more frequently than (top) public administrators. One could say that this *should* be the case, as the machinery of governance is not neutral (Heath 2020). There are clear differences between top public administrators and aldermen in the extent to which values conflicts are perceived. The evidence indicates that aldermen perceive many more value conflicts. Aldermen experience conflicts between performance and procedural values in the governance *process*, as well as in policy *content* and goals. In the seminal study on value conflict in public governance by Thacher and Rein (2004), this distinction is not made; they mainly study value conflict in *public policy*. Values such as safety, prosperity, and freedom are, to them, "the ultimate ends of public policy" (Thacher and Rein 2004: 460). That means that many of the examples they give of conflicting policy values are values of the policies (and their goals) themselves.

The next section focuses on empirical research on the *strategies* used by actors and institutions when dealing with such value conflicts as were described in the current section. The next section also points out the advantages and disadvantages of each of these coping strategies. The same five case studies will be revisited, and a literature review conducted to find the answers.

4 Dealing with Value Conflict: Some Coping Strategies

4.1 Introduction

Even though O'Kelly and Dubnick (2005: 393) claim it almost never happens, they believe that "the study of public administration in general should be aimed at analyzing how public administrators make decisions in the face of dilemmas." This is the focus of the VBG perspective and the topic of this section. It is not just about the (un)conscious decisions by actors in public governance, but also about how institutions deal with value conflict.

As has become clear by now, value conflict is a fact of life in public governance. Value conflict, in itself, is not a problem; value conflicts can bring forth change for the better by prompting alertness and innovation. Yet, there is a danger that value conflicts can lead to a state of *paralysis* (Thacher and Rein 2004), to *ineffective* governance, and to *undesirable* outcomes where important public values are lost. Coping strategies (or coping mechanisms, as they are also called in the literature) are used to prevent these pathologies. For example, when in collaborative governance there is a value conflict, "a range of responses and outcomes may unfold, depending on the origins and tractability of the conflict, as well as how the partners cope with it" (Page et al. 2018: 242).

When it comes to the issue of dealing with value conflicts in public governance, Thacher and Rein have made an important theoretical contribution. Conventionally, Thacher and Rein (2004) argue, the response of public actors to value conflicts has been seen as either a matter of balancing competing goals or making a trade-off (famous examples: Okun 1975; Le Grand 1990). The archetype of trade-offs is the cost–benefit analysis: the values are given a monetary value (an economistic approach to values), and the optimum is calculated. But as we saw in Section 2, and as Lukes (1996) has also shown, values can be incommensurable, and not all our choices are to be understood as trade-offs. Thacher and Rein (2004) developed an (empirically grounded) theoretical framework for understanding how value ambiguity is coped with in public governance. They claim that as conflicting values are often not treated as commensurable, a repertoire of alternative strategies is drawn up to enable coping. These public governance strategies should not be confused with the more psychological coping strategies mentioned in the literature for individual (frontline) workers dealing with stressful situations and dealing with policy alienation (cf. Tummers et al. 2013). In the latter case, coping is about the psychology of individuals dealing with a personally stressful situation: "'Coping' is the current term for understanding frontline workers responses to stress" (Tummers et al. 2013: 2). For example, Lipsky showed that civil servants sometimes routinize their actions. Doing so makes life easier, since choices for a particular value have to be made only once, after which it becomes routine. Here, however, coping is not about an agent-based dilemma (Dubbink 2008), but about a strategy for dealing with a public *governance* dilemma.

4.2 Six Different Coping Strategies

Based on a study of the practice of crime policy, retirement policy, and refugee policy, Thacher and Rein (2004: 458) came up inductively with three coping strategies: firewalls, cycling, and casuistry. "To explain how these strategies can be rational, we rely on recent developments in the theory of practical reasoning, which indicate that rationality is often less algorithmic than traditional views have suggested, in that it relies on situated judgments about what is appropriate in particular times, places, and contexts that are difficult to articulate using the instrumentalist framework." Stewart (2006) discusses – in the context of policy change – the three strategies of Thacher and Rein, which she calls processes, and adds three more: hybridization, bias, and incrementalism. The six coping strategies described by Thacher, Rein, and Stewart entail the following approaches.

In *Firewalls*, or structural separation, conflicting values are separated organizationally. Different organizations, departments, or persons are made responsible for the realization of different values. "Conventional government works by dividing up its complex systematic reality into functional chunks, the familiar departments of health, education, industry, and so on" (Stewart 2009). Firewalls turn into a coping strategy if responsibility for pursuing specific values is allocated in isolation to different departments, in theory preventing the value conflict from arising in any department (Steenhuisen and Van Eeten 2008). The advantage of this strategy is that all values receive attention, and the value on which they need to base their action is clear for individuals within a particular organization or department. However, the strategy also has disadvantages. Value conflicts can resurface when the various institutions deal with similar cases. Moreover, although departments can improve the way they realize their own values, the separation of values blocks the chances of integrated learning and can lead to criticism about an inconsistent public sector. An example is environmental policy (Stewart 2006). In many Western governments, separate departments are established to deal with environmental values, whereas production-related departments are not affected and continue with the same policies. Possibilities for learning are thus frustrated. "Australian educational policy provides a good example of this phenomenon. Asymmetrical governance structures derail productive debate because funding and accountability for government and nongovernment schools are separated by federal 'firewalls'" (Stewart 2006: 188).

In *Hybridization*, no value separation occurs. Two distinct policies or practices are allowed to coexist, though they have different value bases (Stewart 2006). The strategy entails combining various conflicting values that might arise, for instance, as a result of additions to earlier policies bringing with them new values. Hybridization can be the result of the "inheritance effect" (Rose and Davies 1994): a new government inherits the policies of the previous one, and then adds layers of its own. "A good example of hybridization is the values mixture that constitutes new public management, as a result of which public servants are meant simultaneously to be professional, efficient, neutral, and responsive. The market-oriented values have been overlaid on top of the more traditional public service ethos to form a hybridized result . . . Work by Pratchett and Wingfield in British local government showed that institutional change allowed the traditional public service ethos to coexist" (Stewart 2006: 188). Another example comes from environmental and climate policies. "From the values perspective, sustainable development represents a hybrid paradigm – a way of encompassing the values of both greenness and growth. The paradigm is an attempt to 'inscribe' one value in terms of the other" (Stewart 2009: 154). Hybridization is the strategy most in line with a positive appreciation of value conflict: hybridizations might lead to innovative solutions by those public actors who execute such policies, and all values are made important in discourses and rhetoric. The downside is that the public actors executing the policy are not able to balance the different values in their daily work.

Casuistry is a form of moral taxonomy reasoning (Jonsen and Toulmin 1988) that allows value conflicts to be transcended, using analogical reasoning. A decision is made for each particular value conflict based on experiences in similar cases. As Thacher and Rein (2004) explain, casuistry means that one does not decide by reasoning deductively, but rather by reasoning analogically and comparing a case to similar ones. "In social welfare policy, an important strand of thinking holds that professionals should have wide discretion to decide what resources the beneficiaries of public programs should get so that they can make context-specific judgments about what is appropriate in the situation... in foreign policy Weiner explicitly calls for a casuistical response to the dilemmas that arise in refugee crises" (Thacher and Rein 2004: 477). Thacher and Rein go on to give the example of the police. The police can use violence to handle criminals effectively. How to do that without too much violence is often determined by the particular situation of each case. The making of budgets also clearly has a casuistic component, the allocation of resources is a values choice (Stewart 2006). "Politically, governments do not wish to be seen to be robbing Peter to pay Paul, even though this is what they are doing" (Stewart 2006: 189). The advantage of casuistry is that all values are considered by the same public official, and a customized solution can be found in every case. Moreover, as cases are constantly compared, learning can flourish too. However, casuistry puts a lot of pressure on the public official who needs to commit time and energy to come to a good balance in every case.

Incrementalism – or stepped change – entails more and more emphasis being slowly put on one particular value. This strategy can be suitable when there is insufficient information, when the technical complexity is too large, or when nonincremental strategies carry too many significant disadvantages with them (Stewart 2006). By not changing too abruptly, opposition to a particular choice might be mitigated, and those who want something done about the value conflict satisfied; it dampens opposition. However, the fact that changes are only small is precisely the disadvantage of this method: those public officials who oppose these changes might just hold on to their old practices and value preferences.

In *Bias*, a choice is made in favor of one or more of the conflicting values. For example, when some values are no longer recognized as important, taking away the value conflict between these and other values. Stewart (2006) describes how a bias often develops within a policy paradigm or as a result of performance measurements (which reward behavior in line with certain values). A bias results in clarity for both public officials, who know what values they should adhere to, and citizens, who know what they can expect from public officials. However, this strategy also has disadvantages: it leads to feelings of dissatisfaction among those who favor other values, and it might result in suboptimal solutions – or even large scandals – in particular cases where some values are neglected in favor of others. In the scandals described at the beginning of this Element, this became all too clear.

Values can be excluded through two power-related techniques: development of dominant policy paradigms and "technicization" (Stewart 2006). Policy paradigms are discourses that make sense of the world (see Section 2). Public governance takes place within an assumed set of values or paradigms. Paradigms establish the limits of what can and cannot be said in a particular governance context, what Foucault called "the conditions of possibility" of a discourse. Moral questions and the factual images are part of the same discourse (De Graaf 2005). Paradigms can thus subvert values. For example, "The supremacy in Australia and New Zealand of policy advising based on economic rationalism has been extensively noted by commentators (see, for example, Kelsey 1997; Pusey 1991)" (Stewart 2006: 191). Values within a certain paradigm are taken for granted and have a neutral status. Other values – those not in the dominant discourse – are outside the conditions of possibility. And "by 'technicization,' I mean the tendency, partly inevitable, partly chosen, for values conflicts or even differences, to be dealt with by technical means – the 'instrumental rationality' Weber saw as one of the hallmarks of bureaucratic government. In some situations, technicization works by 'crowding out' other values. Over the past 20 years, the values and language of management has had an enormous impact on the public sector in most Organization for Economic Cooperation and Development (OECD) countries" (Stewart 2006: 191). If efficiency is a self-validating goal in public governance, within an economistic policy paradigm, actors can easily overlook the value consequences of this bias, at the expense of values like equity (Stewart 2009: 80).

In the sixth strategy, *Cycling*, conflicting values are attended to sequentially; just as in incrementalism, there is an explicit time element. The values that are considered to be important are pursued for a specific period until resistance leads to them being overturned and other values taken into account again (Thacher and Rein 2004). Thacher and Rein (2004) give the example of crime policy; many police departments know the tension between completely committing to crime control and community relations – as was demonstrated in the case study involving the police in Section 3 – cycling between liberty and order. "Policy flip-flops occur repeatedly in criminal justice systems, because the consequences of tough-mindedness overload the goals, while the consequences of tender-mindedness produce the conditions for a conservative backlash" (Stewart 2009: 95). In the social security domain, cycling strategies are also often found – think of the three scandals at the beginning of this Element. Lipsky wrote about the "fundamental service dilemma": "how to provide individual responses or treatment on a mass basis" (Lipsky 1980: 44). An efficient system that awards benefits will more easily ignore individual circumstances. This can lead to public outrage and scandals, leading to changes in the system with more attention being paid to individual cases – until the system is considered too expensive and is made more efficient again, etcetera. The advantage of cycling is that it prevents the paralyzing effect a value conflict can have and thus offers room for innovation. Combining the various new ideas that originate in periods in which different values have a central role can result in innovative solutions that stimulate a balance between different values. The disadvantage is that there is no guarantee that these new solutions are indeed better: while a temporary focus on value A might make an organization more capable of realizing that value, it also makes the organization less capable of realizing value B.

4.3 Further Strategies

It is important to note that Thacher and Rein identified their strategies inductively; they are not based on theoretical choices. The six strategies presented in Section 4.2 can thus overlap, and the list can certainly be expanded (Thacher and Rein 2004: 464). In the literature, we find several suggestions for expansion. De Graaf et al. (2016) mention *escalation*, which can be described as shifting conflict to a higher organizational level (Aschhoff and Rick 2018). An opposite strategy is the formulation of *vague policy* (Koppenjan 2022a, 2022b): politicians or top administrators refuse to take difficult decisions and leave the dilemma for policy implementation (Steenhuisen and Van Eeten 2012). Aschhoff and Rick (2018: 786) also describe a different strategy, which they label *regulation*: "fixing formal rules, developing informal rules, and shifting decision making towards citizens provides guidance for collaborative actors in conflict situations." Other examples in the literature include *defining floors*: minimum levels of attention to be paid to certain values, instead of constantly maximizing multiple competing values (Steenhuisen 2009b). And *gag rules*: suppress consideration of the issue that gives rise to the conflict altogether, coping with value conflict by adopting gag rules that restrict the legitimate topics of public debate (Thacher and Rein 2004).

Yet another coping strategy Koppenjan (2022b) mentions is *compensating*. For example, when permission was given to the Schiphol Airport to expand, the local residents received compensation in the form of insulation for their houses to reduce noise disturbance. Another example of compensating is when the extraction of gas in the Dutch province of Groningen led to earthquakes, the damages to private houses were partly compensated for. In this case, it was not a cheap strategy: for every euro paid as compensation for earthquake damage in Groningen, an additional seventy-four cents went to the bureaucracy to arrange the compensation (Algemene Rekenkamer 2022). Compensation does not always have to be in monetary terms: yet another (negative) example of compensating arises from the construction of the Tweede Maasvlakte (an extension of the harbor of Rotterdam). The construction destroyed a nature reserve. Part of the plan was to restore the flora and fauna in another area, the so-called Voordelta. The loss of the valued nature reserve was to be compensated by establishing nature somewhere else. This never materialized.

In a recent study by Oldenhof, Wehrens, and Bal (2022) on strategies used in policy experiments that join multiple stakeholders in the co-design, experimentation, implementation, and evaluation of innovative policy ideas in local settings, six new strategy labels are used. These strategies are arrived at through an abductive process of moving back and forth between empirical results and theoretical notions of values strategies and (conflicting) values. This led to six strategies that allow actors to deal with emerging values conflicts: *colonization*, the durable imposition of a dominant valuation scheme on other valuation practices; *prioritization*, choosing to make certain valuation schemes temporarily more important than others; *pilotification*, circumventing tensions between valuation schemes by creating a niche outside the system; *shortcutting*, aligning valuation schemes by strategically selecting the "right" actors to create more convergence between various perspectives; *compromising*, allowing a concession that leads to a (temporary) settlement between multiple valuation schemes; and *enmeshing*, setting up hybrid organizational bodies representing different valuation schemes.

It is worth noting that these abductively obtained strategies show many similarities with the six strategies earlier introduced and most frequently used in the literature. There are clear parallels between colonization and bias, prioritization and cycling, pilotification and firewalls, shortcutting and casuistry (albeit a specific type by selecting specific actors), and between both compromising and enmeshing, and hybridization. The authors state that rather than adding new strategies to an increasing list, they prefer to study how various strategies relate to each other and on what level. They prefer the six new strategies because they "operate on a less abstract organizational meso-level" (Oldenhof, Wehrens, and Bal 2022: 25). Yet they also acknowledge that when frequently applied and over time, meso-level strategies can have macro-level impact.

Reflecting on the character of the various strategies, it is noticeable that they differ conceptually. First of all, while some coping mechanisms are conscious reactions to the conflicts experienced (such as casuistry), others – such as cycling – seem to originate from a series of choices made over time. As a result, it seems likely that cycling will only be found in a longitudinal study of a particular issue.

Secondly, while some are more likely to be on the meso or organizational level – like creating firewalls – others are more likely to be on a micro or personal coping level – for example, bias – or on a macro (system) level. Several of the strategies – such as hybridization – have examples in the micro, meso, and macro levels. This is important to be aware of, as it also means that multiple coping strategies might be used in response to a single value conflict. For instance, one can imagine that creating firewalls on an organizational level could result in a bias for the actors in one of the "firewalled" departments. Also, Stewart (2006), Thatcher and Rein (2004), and Steenhuisen and Van Eeten (2008) relate the coping strategies mainly to policy decisions. Most examples they give concern cases in which different outcome values are in conflict, for instance, punctuality and the safety of trains.

4.4 Avoiding and Embracing Value Conflict

In the context of value conflicts in public innovation, Meijer and De Jong (2020) place strategies aimed at managing value conflicts on a spectrum. At one end is avoidance: organizations can use *denial* (ignore the conflict and its stakeholders) or *hiding* (actively hide the conflict from stakeholders to avoid controversy). This resembles the *formulation of vague policy* strategy. On paper, political actors come to a compromise, thus satisfying the need to come to an agreement, even though the compromise contains hidden values conflicts that are left to policy implementation. In a coalition government system – in which, despite societal polarization, constant political majorities are needed – this coping strategy seems to be used more and more. Creating large problems in policy execution, of course. Avoidance strategies are closed and conflict-averse and are used where there is low conflict intensity or when there is the conviction that the institution *cannot* manage the conflict.

At the other end of the spectrum are "embracing" strategies that are aimed at learning. Meijer and De Jong mention two: *reconciling* (using the analysis of value conflicts to improve the value proposition of the innovation), and *deliberation* (orchestrating an inclusive public or political discussion about the value conflict). These strategies are open and embrace multiple perspectives.

4.5 Advantages and Disadvantages of the Particular Coping Strategies: And the Conditions Under Which They Operate

In introducing the first six strategies, some advantages and disadvantages of each strategy were mentioned in order to explain what the mechanisms entail. In order to indicate more fully the advantages and disadvantages of these strategies, and also to see what evidence exists about conditions for success, a further literature review was conducted. All known academic studies that include evidence on possible (dis)advantages of coping strategies were studied (Thacher and Rein 2004; Stewart 2006, 2009; Steenhuisen and van Eeten 2008; Steenhuisen 2009b; Steenhuisen and Van Eeten 2012; De Graaf, Huberts, and Smulders 2013, 2016; Aschhoff and Rick 2018; De Graaf and Meijer 2019; De Graaf 2021). Table 1 summarizes the known possible (dis)advantages and conditions for success of each coping strategy.

Table 1 can be used to weigh values and strategies prudently in order to deal with value conflicts in public governance. In the next section – which is on the practice of VBG – more on this.

5 The Value-Based Governance Paradigm

5.1 Managerialism

This Element began with the practice of public governance by discussing three real-life cases of bad governance. Subsequently, the attention has mainly been on the *study* of public governance from the VBG perspective: the concepts and contours of such a perspective, what we know about values in Western public governance – such as which values conflict, and which strategies are available in dealing with these conflicts. In this section, we return to the *practice* of public governance. The aim in this section is to sketch the contours of a *public governance paradigm*, an understanding of what constitutes good public governance and management (Torfing et al. 2020: 1). Public governance paradigms are defined as "a relatively coherent and comprehensive set of norms and ideas about how to govern, organize and lead the public sector" (Torfing et al. 2020: 9). The building blocks of VBG will be discussed. This reasoning is not immediately obvious: "Values matter profoundly in public policy, but their influence is deep-seated rather than obvious" (Stewart 2009: 12). Value-based governance is about bringing the value "rationality" back in, in which intrinsic values are recognized.

Current Western public governance is often described as a matter of "politics of expertise," as technocratic (Fischer 1990). Public governance has become a marketplace of interests and services delivered by public organizations, or by private organizations backed by the government. MacIntyre speaks of managerialism pervading modern society, with a strong narrow-minded focus on the value of effectiveness (MacIntyre 1991; Overeem 2011). Today, we see this dominant management logic reflected in the practice and the discourse of Western public administration. According to sociologist Schinkel (2012),

Table 1 Advantages and disadvantages of coping strategies

Coping strategy	Known possible advantages	Known possible disadvantages	Known conditions
Firewalls (structural separation)	Makes it easy to state an institution's objective.	Frustrates possibilities for (policy) learning.	Works better when the jobs to be done are clearly defined, and there are stable professional paradigms to accompany them. Less when there is a need for constancy across a range of functions.
	Helps ensure that each value has a committed defender – that no important value becomes neglected because the institutions that should pursue it have become sidetracked by concern about other values.	It can produce stress or tensions elsewhere in the system.	In some cases, the values at issue are too deeply intertwined to be able to separate them. In cases like that, conflicting values must be considered simultaneously and within the same institution (e.g., the public wants the police to worry about liberty *in the course of* their attempts to control crime).
	Individual tasks are made manageable, and responsibilities appear clearly demarcated.		Some values are less amenable to being "hardened."

			Each separate institution can only partly and temporarily control how its core values will be defined. Institutions can rarely insulate themselves permanently from the values they try to shed. Some values, in order to strengthen them against emerging value conflicts, are in need of internalization in the culture of practice.
Bias	Produces clarity within the organization or society.	It is at the expense of another value.	
	Can create a feeling of safety as the rules are clear.	Less room for individual judgments. Possible dissatisfaction among employees. Creates inflexibility in the organization. If frontline staff become wedded to certain values, they claim this room in operational practice for their value and make it difficult for managers to adjust priorities over time.	

Table 1 (cont.)

Coping strategy	Known possible advantages	Known possible disadvantages	Known conditions
Casuistry	Ensures that one can always look for the "best" solution in each case.	Time-consuming, more demanding, not efficient.	Frontline staff need to be fully informed about the contingencies that matter. This condition, however, is problematic since real-time information on the contingencies is transitory and, what is more, scattered over so many staff, who act separately in a complex chain of value conflicts.
	As cases are constantly compared: learning can flourish.	May raise stress for actors because it puts pressure on the public official as they must spend a lot of time and energy coming to a good balance in each case.	
Cycling (spiraling)	Attention can be concentrated within a period of time.	No guarantee that it leads to improvement: while a temporary focus on value A might make an organization more capable of realizing that value, it should not make the organization less capable of realizing value B (just as bias).	The possibility of a double-edged sword. In some cases, an iterative process of invention may lead to downward spiraling rather than upward spiraling.

	Prevents the paralyzing effect a value conflict can have. May facilitate innovation and invention of new strategies so that they become progressively more sophisticated in the way they handle the dilemma over time. When agents master cycling, they can make progress toward both values, practicing the art of "spiraling."	Possible high transaction costs.
Hybridization	Satisfies the need for an all-embracing rhetoric.	At the practical level, little guidance for dealing with the conflict is given, which might lead to stress. Officials executing the policy might not be able to balance the different values in their daily work.
	May add new preferences to former practices. Competing perspectives can enrich performance. Might lead to innovative solutions by those public officials who need to execute such policies.	Competing perspectives can disguise bad performance.

Table 1 (cont.)

Coping strategy	Known possible advantages	Known possible disadvantages	Known conditions
Incrementalism (stepped change)	It may represent a way forward when non-incremental change is likely to arouse value conflicts that are difficult to manage; it mitigates opposition to a particular choice and satisfies those who ask for a way out of the value conflict. It eases systems and dampens opposition, while signaling intentions for the longer term.	May run into limits when the relationship between the values of the implementing bureaucracy and those embodied in new policy are at odds. In these situations, entrenched and relatively autonomous bureaucracies may resist even small moves in a direction they consider undesirable. Because the changes are only small, those public officials who oppose these changes might just hold on to their old practices and value preferences.	

pragmatism is dominant in current political and administrative thought and actions. Politics has become problem management. Boutellier (2015) called Western governance a "pragmacracy," whereas Trommel (2019b) speaks of the "managerial state." In policy making of the past decennia, the management perspective has been dominant (Putters 2021).

A characteristic of this managerialism "is its reliance on technical expertise (Fischer 1990) and the science-for-policy model as a source of authoritativeness (Hajer 2009)" (Prettner et al. 2023: 141). Contemporary governments *themselves* often depict governance as a technocratic process (Putters 2021), in the suggestion that there is a straight line between science and policy. For the public it is then no longer clear which value choices are being made. Government often justifies its decisions with technical arguments, not value arguments. Especially in crises, the typical default is to rational policies and practices, which often fall short (Ansell and Boin 2019: 1448; Zavattaro et al. 2021). For example, at the outbreak of the COVID-19 pandemic, an Outbreak Management Team (OMT) was assembled to provide scientific input for the Dutch government. All the members of OMT were medical experts (such as virologists, epidemiologists, and doctors). One would expect government to weigh all kinds of values involved in combating a pandemic, lockdown regimes, and so on, using the medical and technical OMT advice to predict as accurately as possible the medical outcomes of the different types of measure. Yet most decisions were *justified* on the grounds that the OMT advice was being followed, "leaving commentators wonder about who is truly in charge during the crisis" (Prettner et al. 2021: 7). As if science could tell the governors what to do, all responsibility was placed on the technical advice of the OMT. But every (non-) decision on the Covid-19 policy was loaded with (conflicting) values – for example, in addition to health, the values of personal freedom and economic and social wellbeing needed to be considered. Yet the policy was portrayed as based purely on the advice of the medical OMT council. There is evidence that the Ministry of Health, Wellbeing, and Sports tried to influence the OMT advice. Publicly, the weighing of values – the essence of public governance – did not take place, even though "It is not so much scientific facts in themselves that may offend people, but the (denial of) values associated with these facts ... When knowledge is at stake, so are the values associated with it (Jasanoff 2004; Jasanoff and Simmet 2017; Durnova 2019)" (Prettner et al. 2021: 2–3).

One of the most important factors in the popularity of the technological frame is the enormous value placed by politicians in current Western governance on *optics*. Once problems in a policy are perceived, the reaction is often along the same lines (Putters 2021: 10). The (social) media play an important role. In the Childcare Benefits Scandal, NAV Scandal, and Robodebt, for example, it was pressure from the media that made the legislator decide to come up with strict anti-fraud laws, just as there was pressure from the politicians and thus the public administrators to keep them in place.

5.2 Technical Rationality Prevents Reflection on Values and Value Conflict

Managerialism leads to the concealing of important values in public governance. In decentralization processes, for example, the assumption of the legislator is often that the weighing of values will take place at the decentralized level, yet this is often not the case (Fleurke, Hulst, and De Vries 2021; Putters 2021). We see this, for example, in the social domain in the Netherlands where coping with a lack of resources and the existence of complex rules take up all the time of local government officials (Putters 2021: 8). There is little local discourse on values, for example about which groups should receive support, or about the necessary elements of care provision (Putters 2021). The local view is that dealing with lack of funds and complex rules takes up too much time. The assumption of the legislator was that the outsourcing of care and welfare would create the best choices. Yet, in reality, there is a great deal of uncertainty about who – and which groups – can count on help from the government. There is insufficient help and insufficient quality. It is not just the case that decentralizing policy produces differences between municipalities, there is a strong feeling that many who deserve help are not receiving it.

The report *Klem tussen balie en beleid* ("Stuck between Counter and Policy") by a temporary committee of the Dutch Parliament (*Tijdelijke Commissie Uitvoeringsorganisaties*) reveals that many policy-executing organizations have large problems (Koppenjan 2022b). Analyses – among others by Tjeenk Willink (2021) and Putters (2022a) – show that in public governance an instrumental way of thinking is dominant among public administrators and politicians (Koppenjan 2022b). In their discourse, efficiency is the most important public value. Public governance is based on the principles of market, decentralization, and efficiency (Van de Ven 2021). This combination has resulted in fewer public facilities, especially outside the cities (Van de Ven 2021), because public facilities are primarily based on financial viability. When there are not enough passengers, bus lines are cut; when there are not enough users, libraries are closed. This is at the expense of the values that are at the heart of these facilities. Frequently, these values are not weighed. As we saw in the previous section, through a bias on efficiency, values can be excluded through two power-related techniques: development of dominant policy paradigms, and "technicization."

When there is insufficient budget, the emphasis is placed on greater efficiency or on accountability and complicated rules. This often does not resolve the problem, but worsens it. For many citizens, self-reliance is not an option. These citizens need public craftsmanship, sensitive to individual needs, instead of efficiency managers (Putters 2021: 9). Tjeenk Willink: Managers do not like differentiation. That costs money. The replacement of people by ICT systems for financial reasons strengthens that process, personal contact disappears. Algorithms do not know people. The level and positions of functionaries who work with these systems, makes it even harder to take individual cases into account. The premise that bigger is better and cheaper, has promoted larger scale operation (translated from Dutch, Tjeenk Willink 2021: 115–16).

A common claim about modern Western society is the Weberian claim that Wertrationalität (value-rationality) is crowded out by Zweckrationalität (purpose-rationality) (Van Putten 2020: 59). In value-rationality, social action is motivated "by a conscious belief in the – ethical, aesthetic religious, or however indicated – absolute intrinsic value of motivated Sichverhalten ('inner behavior') purely as such and independent of success." Whereas purpose-rationality is social action motivated by achieving specific external goals, about selecting the means of achieving specific goals as efficiently as possible. Purpose-rationality rationality is about efficiency (Starke, Heckler, and Mackey 2018); "doing things the right way," rather than "doing the right things" (Adams and Balfour 2004: 143). Fischer (1990) contrasts technical rationality with value rationality and shows that technical rationalism is based on the neglect of normative reasoning.

Zavattaro et al. (2021: 1449): "Conflicting values are difficult for technical rationality to appreciate, so there is a reliance on order and structure offered by tenets of technical rationality" (Spicer 2009; Starke, Heckler, and Mackey 2018). The technical rational perspective in governance is often accompanied by pragmatism – don't rant but brush – and comes at the expense of *reflection* on values and on the legitimacy of choices. Spicer (2010: 64):

> The rhetoric of instrumental rationalism in public administration devalues moral responsibility because it deflects the attention of administrators away from the fact that they must often face difficult choices about competing and incommensurable moral ends. It hides moral choices from the view of administrators by focusing their attention single-mindedly on technical questions about how best to accomplish some predefined sets of measurable goals, missions, or ends.

This tendency is strengthened by AI developments in Western governance. Algorithms, in which the moral dimension is hidden, are being used more and more. Technical rationality does not mean that value conflicts are eliminated, but that certain values are institutionalized and the value conflicts are hidden. Techniques that are presented as value-neutral, in fact, conceal value priorities. Stewart (2006: 192) remarks that economic managerialism in public governance produces a pragmatic kind of change without major value disruption, "a source of major disappointment to many environmentalists." Technical rationality shapes the judgment of values in the policy process, resulting in certain value priorities, yet giving them a neutral status.

Through the emphasis on rational management in governance and the outsourcing of public functions, the practice of policy execution moves further out of sight. As a consequence, citizens increasingly question the *honesty* and *trustworthiness* of government (Putters 2021: 8). Putters (2021) gives several concrete examples of policy areas where the weighing of values did not take place because the state wanted to operate efficiently and in a businesslike manner. For example, a policy through which status holders (refugees) should find jobs quickly and become part of the host society. This group was supposed to assume most of the responsibility for their own integration. Yet many status holders found it difficult to make such a good start: fleeing one's country often has serious consequences for mental health. The status holders were responsible for finding their own language schools. They often chose a language school that did not fit with their level of proficiency in Dutch. Many language schools delivered low-quality and took advantage of the newcomers' inexperience and lack of knowledge. During policy evaluations, everyone agreed that reliance on the self-sustainability of the refuges just wasn't working. In the new integration policy of January 1, 2022, there is more guidance from municipalities and less emphasis on market principles. In the old policy, the weighing of values was neglected, and fundamental questions about refugees, solidarity, and cultural differences were simply overlooked. One result of this was that the policy was ineffective – it did not reach its goals.

5.3 Fact Fetishism

As stated here many times, governance is about values, which is also what Hodgkinson (1978) meant when he stated that governing is philosophy in action (Rutgers 2011). The appraisal (valuing) of information is an essential part of the work of a public functionary (Rutgers 2011). Yet even though values play such a big role in public governance, in the previous two sections, we saw that through managerialism with its technical rationality, values are forced into the background. This is reinforced by other factors in Western societies. Rutgers (2011) speaks about "fact fetishism" to indicate that normative considerations generally stay out of sight, and that where possible, value issues are reduced to euros in the budget.

Provis (2007: 21) identifies three reasons that issues are less likely to be identified as "ethical" issues in public governance. The first reason has to do with the cost of resolving ethical issues. As we saw earlier, it is much harder to negotiate values than it is to negotiate interests. Ury et al. (1988: 15): "in general, reconciling interests is less costly than determining who is right." Value issues are put aside to make it easier to come to a compromise. Yet the issues that are put aside can be very important issues, of course.

Second, ethical issues being involved in a conflict make it harder to predict what the outcome of the conflict will be. With the increasing complexity of policy problems – and the increasing interdependency of policy areas, policy levels, and policy actors (Torfing et al. 2012: 1) – public actors may fear adding to unpredictable controversy within governance. Values can be highly sensitive, and addressing them can exacerbate social relations. This harks back to the bias strategy of "technicization" mentioned in Section 4, a power-related technique by dominant policy paradigms: suppressing other values by focusing on the technical. This was also visible in the three scandals at the beginning of this Element.

Third, Provis (2007) claims that identifying issues as ethical issues makes salient the prospect of allocating moral responsibility and blame. This is exactly the reason that politicians prefer avoiding the value dimension and prefer to label issues as "technical" or "economic," as we saw in relation to COVID-19. "To the extent that identifying problems as ethical problems makes salient their potential for leaving some interests or value commitments unsatisfied, it may be that there is an incentive for policy-makers to avoid identifying them in that way" (Provis 2007: 25–26).

Technical problems can be solved by specific expertise, and answers are in terms of "solutions," whereas on value judgments we are all on equal footing and no one can claim decisive expertise (Provis 2007: 27). This means that technocratic governance approaches, like economistic approaches, sweep relevant values under the carpet and shut out those who are not considered experts. "The constant incursion of market-oriented technocratic solutions to policy problems thus tends constantly to restrict opportunity for argument and discussion about values" (2007: 27).

5.4 The Value-Based Governance Paradigm

So, managerialism, with its technical rationality, and other factors force the values in the practice of public governance into the background. What is needed in the VBG paradigm is to bring the values to the fore, have open dialogue, and weigh the values prudently. Johnson (1993) maintains that ethical thinking is not a step-by-step algorithmic process, but an imaginative act of pattern recognition. So, the pattern recognition processes of moral imagination need to be stimulated in order to recognize, deal with, and weigh values.

The VBG paradigm is about *identifying values in public governance and dealing prudently with tensions between (potentially) conflicting values*. Prudently, because it requires acting both with care and acting wisely. Care should be taken to bring values to the fore, and then thought is needed to deal with value tensions. The scandals described at the beginning of this Element clearly do not qualify as VBG. After all, there was a paramount bias strategy with a bias on fraud prevention, so much so that other important values were not prudently considered. Neither can managerialism be described as VBG: it barely deals with value tensions, let alone deals with them prudently.

VBG is about the normative dimension – the value-laden basis (Van Steden, Van Putten, and Hoogland 2019) – of public governance; it is about overcoming a technocratic rationality and fact fetishism, and bringing values to the fore. Spicer summarized VBG *avant la lettre*: "public administrators need to go beyond the science-based instrumental rationalism and determinism that characterize too much of our field and to recognize that the management of conflicting values is an essential part of their responsibilities" (Spicer 2010: 10). Politicians and all other public actors should be added to public administrators here.

In VBG, the two principal activities are:

(1) Identifying values and value conflicts
(2) Weighing the values and strategies prudently in order to deal with the value conflicts

The first principal activity of VBG is about reflection on values and value conflict in governance (contrasting with control, as in managerialism). This reflection occurs in a complex modern-day governance in which many different actors play a role; complexity is acknowledged, and uncertainty and unpredictability are embraced. This is similar to what Bussemaker (2020) calls adaptive governance.

Schöne and Rein (1994) published a book on frame reflection in order to deal with intractable policy controversies. They underline the distinction between action and reflection, and call for reflective discourse in mutual assumption, beliefs, and values. Larat and Chauvigné (2017) call for the capacity for reflective analysis to be developed and practical application that will allow a critical distance and celestialized ethical approach. According to Trommel (2019a), good governance is reflexive governance. "Reflexive," here with an x, as in the word *reflex*, reminding us of the dynamics. "Giddens ... argues that reflexivity stands for the increased ability of modern people to reflect on their values, motives and intentions, as well as on the social consequences that may follow from these behavioral drivers." More recently, Van Putten (2020) has called for reflexive governance along these lines.

Ansell and Boin (2019) propose a Pragmatist's approach to crisis management. This approach places great stress on inquiry in a crisis situation. This element sits very well in VBG. Ansell and Boin: "Inquiry, in the Pragmatist sense, calls for a reflexive and deliberative examination of ways to productively address value conflicts. This is a key point of Pragmatism: Decision makers are not just information processors. They must approach situations as creative, moral, and knowledgeable actors" (Ansell and Boin 2019: 1090).

For the second principal activity, the table in the previous section can play an important and helpful role. Once the values and value conflicts are mapped, different ways of dealing with them need to be weighed. What is the current coping strategy and what advantages and disadvantages does it have? What conditions are of importance here? And what are the (dis)advantages of alternative strategies?

5.5 Role Conceptions in VBG

According to Torfing et al. (2020: 169), a public governance paradigm needs internal consistency: actors, departments, and organizational subsystems need to be aligned. And there needs to be a match between the roles of the actors in public governance.

Values are closely related to the identity of individuals and groups (Rutgers 2011: 19). Stewart (2009: 139–40): "One way in which values are related to actions is through professional identity. The values attached to a professional way of life carry an emotional resonance with those who identify with it. The realities of change are always political in this sense – they signal a reassignment of the right to define what is valuable." Like any governance paradigm, VBG expects a certain role and role conception of public actors. An "administrative role" has been defined by Selden, Brewer, and Brudney (1999: 175) as "a cohesive set of job-related values and attitudes that provides the public administrator with a stable set of expectations about his or her responsibilities."

The classic public administrator as envisioned by Max Weber (e.g., 1946) is neutral and predictable, and has unquestioned obedience and loyalty to the elected political authorities in serving the public good (Weber 1946). "According to Weber, administration should be removed from politics and should serve as the neutral servants of their political masters" (Fry and Nigro 1996: 37). In this view, the role of a politician is to give direction to policies; the bureaucrat's role is not to engage in political decision making but to execute the orders of their political superiors (Fry and Nigro 1996).

Scholars have argued on empirical grounds that the image of Weber's public administrator is simply outdated. The ever-changing organizational context, in America and bureaucracies worldwide, changes role perceptions and loyalties (Bovens 1998). The complexity of society's problems, the professionalism of public administration, media influence, citizens' expectations of responsiveness from administrators (Rosenthal 1999), and transformed constituencies and increased policy volatility (Durant 1991; Rourke 1991) all play a role in the changing context. Denhardt (1988) has mentioned that public administrators have become more involved in making, as opposed to merely executing, policy; or, as 't Hart and Wille (2002) have phrased it, complementarity and teamwork among elected officials and administrators are important elements of modern discourse on the relationship between politics and administration. O'Leary (2006), in her important study of Guerilla Government, has discussed the reality of bureaucratic politics and pointed to three oft-cited books on the policymaking influence of career public servants: Kaufman's (1960) *The Forest Ranger*, Hirschman's (1970) *Exit, Voice and Loyalty*, and Lipsky's (1980) *Street-Level Bureaucracy*.

Public administrators play a crucial role in VBG. From what was previously argued in this section, in VBG public administrators should *not* be monomaniacal problem solvers, nor neutral policy executors, and certainly should not be focused on optics and preoccupied with the image and political survival of their political superior. Nor should they be found suppressing information to Parliament, as we saw in the three scandals at the beginning of this Element (Koppenjan 2022b: 21). In the Childcare Benefits Scandal it became clear that just a small group around the minister determined the minister's political strategy that was mainly based on a *media perspective* (Frederik 2021: 255), creating a situation in which there is no room for an open mind when a problem arises; the focus is purely on optics and the image of the minister. In addition to loyalty to political superiors, public administrators should have a loyalty to public interest (De Graaf 2011). In VBG, the role conception of administrators is less about the image and protection of the minister and the technical execution of policies, and more about strategic thinking (Putters 2022a). They see themselves as facilitators of adequate value choices:

they focus on the value conflicts and present these to the political executives – weigh *all* the values, not just effectiveness and efficiency, but insights, opinions, and dilemmas too, and present and discuss an overview of this. They weigh the different coping strategies, including the advantages and disadvantages, and conditions. And they make sure the distance between citizens and policy actors is not too large, giving benevolence a place in public governance (De Graaf and Van Asperen 2016). Value-Based Governance is more about people, and less about (policy) measures. Administrators do not operate with an image of citizens as rational calculating beings who have a focus on financial and economic considerations (Putters 2022b).

And for politicians and governors, VBG means less hiding behind scientific and technical analysis, and more focus on explicit value choices and dilemmas. Less focus on their own image, more on good governance.

For governance scholars who desire an advising role in public governance – improving governance – VBG means helping practitioners reflect on the value dimension in their situation. Stewart (2009: 200): "If scholars wish to influence the world of action, they need to engage in a form of reflexive prescription. As defined here this means, firstly, defining how one's own values are located and, finally, advocating a change in the way the system operates so as to produce a shift or rebalancing in the desired direction."

5.6 Institutional Reforms in VBG

As discussed in Section 1, many reforms in Western public governance in the eighties and nineties were inspired by New Public Management (NPM) theories. The normative character in daily governance has receded into the background, and efficiency has become the core value (Powell and De Vries 2011). In NPM, management became a value in itself (Ringeling 2017: 27) and the market is central: steering, not rowing (Osborne and Gaebler 1992). When value conflicts appear, a bias strategy for efficiency is usually chosen (see Section 4). A clear disadvantage of a bias strategy is that the choice of one value is at the cost of other – in this case, crucial – public values (Maesschalck 2004; Diefenbach 2009). NPM does not seem to be the best way to get to VBG.

In reforms after NPM in the public sector – inspired by modernistic institutionalism – *network management* took center stage (Bevir 2010). Successful networks would demand cooperation, negotiation, flexibility, and trust. In case of value conflicts within this perspective, parties need to negotiate a trade-off between their interests. A first problem for VBG is that values are wrongly seen and treated as commensurable, with the consequence that important public values are pushed, unseen, into the background.

Also, because of the increasing complexity of governance and the dependence on other actors in networks, it is harder and harder to hold actors in public governance accountable (Bevir 2010). Accountability by whom and to whom? Governance becomes (too) complex: the State no longer has an overview of service delivery. The worries that then arise about the value of *quality* lead to strategies that resemble firewalls: specific organizations are made responsible for guarding the value of quality, as we saw in the case of academic teachers in Sections 3 and 4. Making governance even more complex and leading to an explosion of audits, regulatory agencies, oversight, regulations, and benchmarks (Sent 2014). Moran (2003) speaks of a regulatory state, with an ever-increasing number of specialized actors in public governance having diffused power. One of many examples would be the abolition of national student grants in the Netherlands. Students were promised that the money saved would be used to improve the quality of Higher Education. To "ensure" that was the case – at a time of austerity, cutbacks, and concomitant heavy teaching loads and high work pressure at universities (De Graaf 2021) – the money was ring-fenced. The result has been that academic departments cannot just use the money to hire extra teaching personnel; program directors need to show how every euro is being used specifically for innovation and quality improvement.

Nowadays, according to Bevir (2010: 177),

> reforms of public policy and the public sector are often inspired by the new theories of governance. To be more precise, they are inspired by rational choice theory, and above all, by mid-level social science associated with the new institutionalism. They neglect more interpretive approaches to social science. As such, they represent a quest for efficiency based on new forms of expertise. They do not pursue participatory, deliberative, or dialogic alternatives.

The collaborative governance practices as described in Section 1 often lead to the question of how to implement policies given the proliferation of markets and networks in the public sector. In order to institutionalize VBG, and thus to deal well with (new) value conflicts in public governance – reforms from the interpretative approach are called for (Bevir 2010), promoting dialogic and deliberative approaches to public governance. The focus is, then, on the social construction of policy networks. Governance consists of contingent, ever-changing, and controversial practices, putting traditional values in another light.

Bevir: "Social scientists often treat self-interest and social norms as both fixed and defined against each other ... The presence of multiple, shifting rationalities suggests ... that we need to think about the new governance not in terms of fixed institutions or clearly defined social trajectories, but in terms of contingent, diverse, and contested practices" (Bevir 2010: 263–64). Bevir (2010) pleads for "participatory practices." This fits well with developments such as collaborative governance (Ansell and Gash 2007), as discussed in Section 1. As far as reforms in public governance go, one can think of juries, citizen forums, or citizen audits: governance arrangements in which citizens not only give their oral input, but also – and this is important – bear (some) responsibility. Or lotteries, instead of elections (Van Reybrouck 2013). These new governance arrangements are better equipped to deal with the value conflicts around democracy and legitimacy, and thus support VBG.

The existing and new participation participatory practices clash with the more traditional representative image of democracy. They bring less *formal* equality and uniformity; participatory practices do not find their legitimacy in the "one person one vote" principle. For VBG, currently, there is too much focus on representative democracy, with too much weight on elections and referenda. Democracy is so much more than elections, and elections are not always the best way to realize democratic values. Instead, when looking for democracy and legitimacy, in VBG the focus is on the transparency of decision processes, participation of relevant valueholders, and the fit between the process and the problem that is addressed (Bevir 2010). Citizens shouldn't just vote every four years; they should participate in the governance process and *bear responsibility* in governance processes. Too often in citizen participation, citizens are (only) involved in the execution of policies, not the formulation of policies; they are not part of the most important value decisions. This must mean more local participation and deliberation practices, where everyone is enabled to introduce values.

6 Summary and Conclusions

The objective of this Element was to build a VBG perspective that brings the values of governance to the fore, and to guide the praxis of governance toward such a VBG. The aim was to make visible the all-important dimension of value in public governance, while sketching a practice of governance in which values take center stage.

In Section 1, the need for a VBG perspective in Public Administration was argued. Section 2 laid down the theoretical groundwork of such a perspective and introduced the epistemology and theoretical framework, looking at how values are made manifest.

In the two sections that followed, the focus was on empirical research from the VBG perspective. In Section 3, a cross-case analysis of five empirical case studies using the VBG perspective was discussed. It provided a first impression of the values that are important and that conflict in Western public governance – *effectiveness*, *efficiency*, *lawfulness*, *transparency*, and *participation* were mentioned often.

The five case studies were all conducted in the Netherlands. Where possible, the outcomes were related to evidence from other Western countries, but as noted earlier, empirical evidence on value in public governance is scarce. More evidence is needed, and especially more international comparative research, if we are to fill in the picture. Van der Wal (2016: 3) called earlier for more studies on this, "in order to make more robust claims about which public values are really most important and why." Such research would be beneficial, not just to reflect what prevails in different countries, but also in different professions and different contexts. The case studies made clear that the differences in professions and contexts are highly influential on the importance of specific values and on which values conflict.

All of this leads to an agenda for future research that adopts the VBG perspective. *Which values play a role in Western public governance, which values conflict, what are the conditions that influence these conflicts in different professions and contexts, and what are the different value profiles of the different actors?*

As became clear in this Element, value conflict is a fact of life in public governance. Value conflict, in itself, is not a problem; value conflicts can bring forth change for the better by prompting alertness and innovation. Yet, there is a danger that value conflicts can lead to a state of *paralysis* (Thacher and Rein 2004), to *ineffective* governance, and to *undesirable* outcomes where important public values are lost. Coping strategies are used to prevent these pathologies.

A cross-case analysis of the five cases examined in Section 4 revealed that bias is the most-used coping strategy, with hybridization and firewalls completing the top three strategies. This leads to the proposition that these are the most-used coping strategies in Western governance and adds to the research agenda to study whether this proposition is actually the case in different countries, professions, and contexts. Such research would also provide evidence on what works best in the different countries, professions, and contexts. It is not just the frequency with which strategies are applied that is of interest, but also the drivers that determine which strategies are chosen and the factors and conditions that influence their success. According to Koppenjan (2022b: 19–20), we do not yet know the extent to which – and under which circumstances – coping strategies lead to adequate value choices. There has not been much research on this.

This prompts the following addition to the research agenda involving the VBG perspective: *Which coping strategies are used in different settings of governance and in which different combinations? What are the drivers/institutional conditions determining the choice of strategy in public governance? And what works and under what conditions?*

Some coping strategies are deliberate, others are not. By describing particular value conflicts and increasing our knowledge on coping strategies in specific cases, valueholders can be made aware of the strategies that are currently used, as well as the advantages, disadvantages, and known conditions for success, and the way in which value conflict is currently dealt with can be better known and understood.

In the literature, there is some evidence of this research agenda to be found, especially in the literature on policy change. The concept of policy paradigms plays an important role here. "Policy paradigms have been defined as sets of ideas that make sense of the world, and, along with power, organization, and policy itself, one of the four constitutive dimensions of governing arrangements in a specific issue area" (Stewart 2006: 190). For example, it has been maintained here that hybridization is prevalent in academic teaching. Evans (2023: 4) states that bias "is commonly observed in the environmental policy domain."

In Section 5, we returned to the *practice* of public governance: the contours of the VBG paradigm were sketched, namely, public governance with normative reasoning. Value-based governance was defined as *governance which prudently deals with tensions between (potentially) conflicting values*.

VBG is morally important: in the first section, we saw that there is much power in public governance, and the impact on everyone's lives is enormous. There can be no non-arbitrary way of making choices among values (Stewart 2006), and yet there is hardly any weighing of values going on in public governance. Currently in public governance, the deliberation about values remains under the radar (Putters 2021). And as we know from the three scandals, things can go horribly wrong when value conflicts are not dealt with prudently (Koppenjan 2022b). When the focus is on (conflicting) *interest*, there is a tendency to view governance as a zero-sum game. This tendency is much smaller when values are central: as we saw, values can hardly be understood in terms of trade-offs. The purpose of public governance is to *realize* values.

In VBG, the two principal activities are:

(1) Identifying values and value conflicts
(2) Weighing the values and strategies prudently in order to deal with the value conflicts

The first principal activity of VBG is reflection on values and value conflict in governance (contrasting with control, as in managerialism). This reflection occurs in a complex modern-day governance in which many different actors play a role; complexity is acknowledged, and uncertainty and unpredictability are embraced.

For the second principal activity, the table in Section 4 – which presents the advantages and disadvantages of different strategies, and their known conditions – can play an important and helpful role. The table can be used to weigh values and strategies prudently in order to deal with value conflicts in public governance. Once the values and value conflicts are mapped, different ways of dealing with them need to be weighed. What is the current coping strategy and what advantages and disadvantages does it have? What conditions are of importance here? And what are the (dis)advantages of alternative strategies?

In VBG, *learning* strategies play an important role. Strategies such as reconciliation and deliberation are very explicit about value conflict and thus put value conflict to constructive use (Meijer and De Jong 2020). This is helpful in creating sustainable solutions to value conflicts (Steenhuisen 2009b; Meijer and De Jong 2020).

References

Adams, Guy B., and Danny L. Balfour. 2004. *Unmasking Administrative Evil* (M.E. Sharpe: New York).

Algemene_Rekenkamer. 2022. "Resultaten verantwoordingsonderzoek 2021 Ministerie van Economische Zaken en Klimaat." https://www.rekenkamer.nl/onderwerpen/verantwoordingsonderzoek/documenten/rapporten/2022/05/18/resultaten-verantwoordingsonderzoek-2021-ministerie-van-economische-zaken-en-klimaat. Retrieved: 30 August 2022.

Alvesson, Mats, and Dan Karreman. 2000. "Varieties of Discourse: On the Study of Organizations through Discourse Analyses," *Human Relations*, 53: 1125–49.

Ansell, Chris, and Arjen Boin. 2019. "Taming Deep Uncertainty: The Potential of Pragmatist Principles for Understanding and Improving Strategic Crisis Management," *Administration & Society*, 51: 1079–112.

Ansell, Chris, and Alison Gash. 2007. "Collaborative Governance in Theory and Practice," *Journal of Public Administration Research and Theory*, 18: 543–71.

Ansell, Chris, and Jacob Torfing. 2018. *How Does Collaborative Governance Scale?* (Bristol University Press: Bristol).

Aschhoff, Nils, and Rick Vogel. 2018. "Value Conflicts in Co-Production: Governing Public Values in Multiactor Settings," *International Journal of Public Sector Management*, 31: 775–93.

Bailey, Stephan. 1964. "Ethics and the Public Life," *Public Administration Review*, 24: 234–43.

Beck Jørgensen, Torben. 2006. "Public Values, Their Nature, Stability and Change: The Case of Denmark," *Public Administration Quarterly*, 30: 365–98.

Beck Jørgensen, Torben, and Barry Bozeman. 2007. "Public Values. An Inventory," *Administration & Society*, 39: 354–81.

Beck Jørgensen, Torben, and Mark Rutgers. 2015. "Public Values: Core of Confusion? Introduction to the Centrality and Puzzlement of Public Values Research," *American Review of Public Administration*, 45: 3–12.

Beck Jørgensen, Torben, and Ditte-Lene Sørensen. 2013. "Codes of Good Governance: National or Global Values?" *Public Integrity*, 15: 71–96.

Beck Jørgensen, Torben, and Karsten Vrangbæk. 2011. "Value Dynamics: Towards a Framework for Analyzing Public Value Changes," *International Journal of Public Administration*, 34: 486–96.

Berglund, Nina. 2019. "NAV Scandal Linked to EØS Ignorance: News in English," *NEWSinENGLISH.no*.

2020. "NAV Scandal Leaves No One Accountable," *NEWSinENGLISH.no*.

Berlin, Isaiah. 1982. *Against the Current: Essays in the History of Ideas* (Hogarth Press: London).

1992. *The Crooked Timber of Humanity* (Vintage Brooks: New York).

Bevir, Mark. 2010. *Democratic Governance* (Princeton University Press: Princeton).

2012. *Governance: A Very Short Introduction* (Oxford University Press: Oxford).

Bøgh Andersen, Lotte, Torben Beck Jørgensen, Anne Mette Kjeldsen, Lene Holm Pedersen, and Karsten Vrangbæk. 2012. "Public Value Dimensions: Developing and Testing a Multi-Dimensional Classification," *International Journal of Public Administration*, 35: 715–28.

Boltanski, Luc, and Laurent Thévenot. 1999. "The Sociology of Critical Capacity," *European Journal of Social Theory*, 2: 359–77.

2006. *On Justification: Economies of Worth* (Princeton University Press: Princeton).

Boutellier, Hans. 2011. *De improvisatiemaatschappij: Over de sociale ordening van een onbegrensde wereld* (Boom Lemma uitgevers: Den Haag).

2015. *Het seculiere experiment* (Boom: Amsterdam).

Bovaird, Tony. 2007. "Beyond Engagement and Participation: User and Community Coproduction of Public Services," *Public Administration Review*, 67: September–October: 846–60.

Bovaird, Tony, and Elke Löffler. 2003. "Evaluating the Quality of Public Governance: Indicators, Models and Methodologies," *International Review of Administrative Sciences*, 69: 313–28.

Bovaird, Tony, Gregg Van Ryzin, Elke Loeffler, and Salvador Parrado. 2015. "Activating Citizen to Participate in Collective Co-Production of Public Services," *Journal of Social Policy*, 44: 1–23.

Bovens, Mark. 1998. *The Quest for Responsibility* (Cambridge University Press: Cambridge).

Bovens, Mark A. P., and Paul 't Hart. 1996. *Understanding policy fiascoes* (Transaction: New Brunswick).

Bowman, James S., and Clair Connolly Knox. 2008. "Ethics in Government: No Matter How Long and Dark the Night," *Public Administration Review*, 68: 627–39.

Bozeman, Barry. 2002. "Public-Value Failure: When Efficient Markets May Not Do," *Public Administration Review*, 62: 145–61.

2007. *Public Values and Public Interest* (Georgetown University Press: Washington).

Bozeman, Barry, and Japera Johnson. 2015. "The Political Economy of Public Values: A Case for the Public Sphere and Progressive Opportunity," *The American Review of Public Administration*, 45: 61–85.

Brandsen, Taco, and Marlies Honingh. 2015. "Distinguishing Different Types of Coproduction: A Conceptual Analysis Based on the Classical Definitions," *Public Administration Review*, 76: 427–35.

Brandsen, Taco, Trui Steen, and Bram Verschuere (eds.). 2018. *Co-Production and Co-Creation: Engaging Citizens in Public Services* (Routledge: London).

Braun, Caelesta, Menno Fenger, Paul 't Hart, Judith Van der Veer, and Tanja Verheij. 2015. "Qua vadis, Nederlandse Bestuurskunde?" *Bestuurskunde*, 24: 82–92.

Brecht, Arnold. 1959. *Political Theory: The Foundations of Twentieth-Century Political Thought* (Princeton University Press: Princeton).

Bryson, John M., Barbara C. Crosby, and Laura Bloomberg. 2014. "Public Value Governance: Moving beyond Traditional Public Administration and the New Public Management," *Public Administration Review*, 74: 445–56.

Bryson, John M., Bert George, and Danbi Seo. 2024. "Understanding Goal Formation in Strategic Public Management: A Proposed Theoretical Framework," *Public Management Review*, 26: 539–64.

Bussemaker, Jet. 2020. "Van technocratie naar beleid met een hart," *S&D*, 77: 56–65.

Clark, Benjamin, Jeffrey Brudney, and Sung-Gheel Jang. 2013. "Coproduction of Government Services and the New Information Technology: Investigating the Distributional Biases," *Public Administration Review*, 73: 687–701.

Dahl, Robert A. 1947. "The Science of Public Administration: Three Problems," *Public Administration Review*, 7: 1–11.

De Bruijn, Hans. 2011. *"Framing". Over de macht van taal in de politiek.*

De Bruijn, Hans De, and W. Dicke. 2006. "Strategies for Safeguarding Public Values in Liberalized Utility Sectors," *Public Administration*, 84: 717–35.

De Graaf, Gjalt. 1996. "Bestuurskunde is waarde-loos," Erasmus University Rotterdam.

2001. "Business Ethics and Discourse Theory: The Case of Bankers' Conceptualizations of Customers," *Journal of Business Ethics*, 31: 299–319.

2005. "Veterinarians' Discourses on Animals and Clients," *Journal of Agricultural and Environmental Ethics*, 18: 557–78.

2011. "The Loyalties of Top Public Administrators," *Journal of Public Administration Research and Theory*, 21: 285–306.

2016. *Conflicterende waarden in academia* (Inaugural lecture Vrije Universiteit Amsterdam: Amsterdam).

2021. "Value Conflicts in Academic Teaching," *Teaching Public Administration*, 39: 107–24.

De Graaf, Gjalt, and Hester Paanakker. 2022. "Dilemmas and Craftmanship Practices: Strategies for Empirically Uncovering Values and Value Conflicts," in Gry Espedal, Beate Løvaas Jelstad, Stephen Sirris, and Arild Wæraas (eds.), *Researching Values: Methodological Approaches for Understanding Values Work in Organizations and Leadership* (Palgrave Macmillan: Oslo), pp. 93–113.

De Graaf, Gjalt, and Zeger Van der Wal. 2008. "On Value Differences Experienced by Sector Switchers," *Administration & Society*, 40: 79–103.

De Graaf, Gjalt, and Zeger Van der Wal. 2017. "Without Blinders: Public Values Scholarship in Political Science, Economics, and Law: Content and Contribution to Public Administration," *Public Integrity*, 19: 196–218.

De Graaf, Gjalt, Michel Hoenderboom, and Pieter Wagenaar. 2010. "Constructing Corruption," in Gjalt De Graaf, P. von Maravic, and Pieter Wagenaar (eds.), *The Good Cause: Theoretical Perspectives on Corruption* (Budrich: Opladen), pp. 98–114.

De Graaf, Gjalt, Leo Huberts, and Remco Smulders. 2013. *Publieke waarden. De beginselen van goed bestuur in de dagelijkse praktijk van ziekenhuis en gemeente* (Het Ministerie van Binnenlandse Zaken en Koninkrijksrelaties: Den Haag).

2016. "Coping with Public Value Conflicts," *Administration & Society*, 48: 1101–27.

De Graaf, Gjalt, and Albert Meijer. 2013. "De nieuwe netwerksamenleving en openbaar bestuur. Wat Landsmeer ons leert over onze bestuurlijke toekomst," *Bestuurskunde*, 22: 101–6.

2019. "Social Media and Value Conflicts: An Explorative Study of the Dutch Police," *Public Administration Review*, 79: 82–92.

De Graaf, Gjalt, and Hester Paanakker. 2015. "Good Governance: Performance Values and Procedural Values in Conflict," *American Review of Public Administration*, 45: 635–52.

De Graaf, Gjalt, and Hanneke Van Asperen. 2016. "The Art of Good Governance: How Images from the Past Provide Inspiration for Modern Practice," *International Review of the Administrative Sciences*, 84: 405–20.

De Graaf, Gjalt, and Zeger Van der Wal. 2010. "Managing Conflicting Public Values: Governing with Integrity and Effectiveness," *American Review of Public Adminisration*, 40: 623–30.

De Vries, Michiel S. 2002. "Can You Afford Honesty?: A Comparative Analysis of Ethos and Ethics in Local Government," *Administration & Society*, 34: 309–34.

Deleuze, Gilles, and Felix Guattari. 1994. *What Is Philosophy?* (Columbia University Press: New York).

Denhardt, Kathryn G. 1988. *The Ethics of Public Service, Resolving Moral Dilemmas in Public Organizations* (Greenwood Press: Westport).

Diefenbach, Thomas 2009. "New Public Management in Public Sector Organizations: The Dark Sides of Managerialistic 'Enlightenment'," *Public Administration*, 87: 829–909.

Du Gay, Paul. 1996. *Consumption and Identity at Work* (Sage: London).

Dubbink, Wim. 2008. "A Typology of Ethical Problems," *Ethical Perspectives*, 25: 683–714.

Dunleavy, Patrick, Helen Margetts, Simon Bastow, and Jane Tinkler. 2006. "New Public Management Is Dead – Long Live Digital-Era Governance," *Journal of Public Administration Research and Theory*, 16: 467–494.

Durant, Robert F. 1991. "Whither Bureaucratic Influence a Cautionary Note," *Journal of Public Administration Research and Theory*, 1: 461–76.

Durnova, Anna F. 2019. *Understanding Emotions in Post-factual Politics: Negotiating Truths* (Edward Elgar: Cheltenham).

Easton, David. 1965. *A Systems Analysis of Political Life* (Wiley: New York).

Espedal, Gry, Beate Jelstad Lovaas, Stephen Sirris, and Arild Waeraas. 2021. "Researching Values in Organizations and Leadership: Introduction," in Gry Espedal (ed.), *Researching Values in Organizations and Leadership*.

Espedal, Gry, Beate Jelstad Lovaas, Stephen Sirris, and Arild Waeraas. 2022. *Researching Values: Methodological Approaches for Understanding Values Work in Organisations and Leadership* (Palgrave Macmillan: Oslo).

Evans, Megan. 2023. "Backloading to Extinction: Coping with Values Conflict in the Administration of Australia's Federal Biodiversity Offset Policy," *Australian Journal of Public Administration*: 82(2): 1–20.

Februari, Maxim. 2020. "Het dashboard stelt ons voor morele keuzes," *NRC*, May 26.

Fischer, Frank. 1980. *Politics, Values and Public Policy: The Problem of Methodology* (Westview Press: Boulder).

1990. *Technocracy and the Politics of Expertise* (Sage: London).

2005. "Participatory Governance as Deliberative Empowerment: The Cultural Politics of Discursive Space," *American Review of Public Administration*, 36: 19–40.

Fisher, Roger, and William Ury. 1981. *Getting to Yes* (Penguin: London).

Fiske, Alan Page, and Philip E. Tetlock. 1997. "Taboo Trade-offs: Reactions to Transactions that Transgress the Spheres of Justice," *Political Psychology*, 18: 255–97.

Fleurke, Fred, Rudie Hulst, and Piet De Vries. 2021. *Effecten van decentralisatie: Een analyse van zestien bestuurlijke stelsels* (Boom bestuurskunde: Den Haag).

Forester, John. 2009. *Dealing with Differences* (Oxford University Press: New York).

Foucault, Michel. 1977. *Discipline and Punish: The Birth of the Prison* (Vintage: New York).

Frederik, Jesse. 2021. *Zo hadden we het niet bedoeld: De tragedie achter de toeslagenaffaire* (De correspondent: Amsterdam).

Fry, Brian, and Lloyd Nigro. 1996. "Max Weber and US Public Administration: The Administrator as Neutral Servant," *Journal of Management History*, 2 (1): 37–46.

Fukumoto, Eriko, and Barry Bozeman. 2019. "Public Values Theory: What Is Missing?" *American Review of Public Adminisration*, 49: 635–48.

Gawthrop, Luis C. 1998. *Public Service and Democracy: Ethical Imperatives for the 21st Century* (Seven Bridges Press: New York).

Giddens, Anthony. 1981. *A Contemporary Critique of Historical Materialism* (Macmillan: London).

Gray, Barbara, and Jill Purdy. 2018. *Collaborating for Our Future: Multistakeholder Partnerships for Solving Complex Problems* (Oxford University Press: Oxford).

Gregory, Robert J. 1999. "Social Capital Theory and Administrative Reform: Maintaining Ethical Probity in Public Service," *Public Administration Review*, 59: 63–76.

Haidt, Jonathan. 2012. *The Righteous Mind: Why Good People Are Divided by Politics and Religion* (Pantheon: New York).

Hajer, Maarten. 1995. *The Politics of Environmental Discourse* (Clarendon Press: Oxford).

Hajer, Maarten. 2009. *Authoritative Governance: Policy Making in the Age of Mediatization* (Oxford University Press: Oxford).

Hampshire, Stuart 1983. *Morality and Conflict* (Harvard University Press: Cambridge, MA).

Hart, Paul 't, and Anchrit W. Wille (eds.). 2002. *Politiek-ambtelijke verhoudingen in beweging* (Boom: Amsterdam).

Haynes, Philip. 2018. "Understanding the Influences of Values in Complex Systems-Based Approaches to Public Policy and Management," *Public Management Review*, 20: 980–96.

Heath, Joseph. 2020. *The Machinery of Government: Public Administration and the Liberal State* (Oxford University Press: New York).

Hinman, Lawrence M. 2013. *Ethics: A Pluralistic Approach to Moral Theory*. 5th Ed. International Edition (Cengage Learning: Wadsworth).

Hirschman, Albert O. 1970. *Exit, Voice and Loyalty: Responses to Decline in Firms, Organizations, and States* (Cambridge University Press: Cambridge).

Hodgkinson, Christopher 1978. *Towards a Philosophy of Administration* (St. Martin's Press: New York).

Hood, Christopher C. 1991. "A Public Management for all Seasons?" *Public Administration*, 69: 3–20.

Hood, Christopher. 1995. "The 'New Public Management' in the 1980s: Variations on a Theme," *Accounting, Organizations and Society*, 20: 93–109.

Huberts, Leo W. J. C., D. Pijl, and A. Steen. 1999. "Integriteit en corruptie," in C. Fijnaut, E. Muller, and U. Rosenthal (eds.), *Politie. Studies over haar werking en organisatie* (Samson: Alphen aan den Rijn), 433–72.

Huberts, Leo, André van Montfort, Alan Doig, and Denis Clark. 2006. "Rule-making, Rule-breaking? Law Breaking by Government in the Netherlands and the United Kingdom," *Crime, Law & Social Change*, 46: 133–59.

Ianniello, Mario, Silvia Iacuzzi, Paolo Fedele, and Luca Brusatie. 2019. "Obstacles and Solutions on the Ladder of Citizen Participation: A Systematic Review," *Public Management Review*, 21(1): 21–46, Online First.

Innes, Judith E., and David E. Booher. 2018. *Planning with Complexity: An Introduction to Collaborative Rationality for Public Policy* (Routledge: London).

Jasanoff, Sheila. 2004. *States of Knowledge: The Co-production of Science and Social Order* (Routledge: London).

Jasanoff, Sheila, and Hilton R. Simmet. 2017. "No Funeral Bells: Public Reason in a 'Post-Truth' Age," *Social Studies of Science*, 47: 751–70.

Johnson, Mark. 1993. *The Moral Imagination* (University Press of Chicago: Chicago).

Jonsen, Albert, and Stephen Toulmin. 1988. *The Abuse of Casuistry* (Harvard University Press: Cambridge, MA).

Kaufman, Herbert. 1960. *The Forest Ranger* (John Hopkins University Press: Baltimore).

Kelsey, Jane. 1997. *The New Zealand Experiment: A World Model for Structural Adjustment?* (Auckland University Press: Auckland).

Kjaer, Anne Mette. 2004. *Governance* (Polity Press: Cambridge).

Klamer, Arjo. 2016. *Doing the Right Thing: A Value Based Economy* (Ubiquity Press: London).

Koppenjan, Joop. 2022a. "Over instrumenteel bestuur en publieke waarden. Wat kunnen we leren van het publieke-waardenperespectief?" *Bestuurskunde*, 31: 38–54.

2022b. "*Van alles is weer waardeloos. Ook de bestuurskunde?*" (Erasmus University Rotterdam: Rotterdam).

Koppenjan, Joop, and Erik-Hans Klijn. 2004. *Managing Uncertainties in Networks* (Routledge: New York).

Larat, Fabrice, and Christian Chauvigné. 2017. "Overcoming the Tensions between Values: A Challenge for French Public Service Managers and Their Training Schools," *International Review of Administrative Sciences*, 83: 463–80.

Le Grand, Julian. 1990. "Equity versus Efficiency: The Elusive Trade-off," *Ethics*, 100: 554–68.

Lindblom, Charles. 1959. "The Science of Muddling Through," *Public Administration Review*, 19: 79–88.

Lipsky, Michael. 1980. *Street-Level Bureaucracy: Dilemmas of the Individual in Public Services* (Russell Sage Foundation: New York).

Lukes, Stephan. 1989. "Making Sense of Moral Conflict," in N. L. Rosenblum (ed.), *Liberalism and the Moral Life* (Harvard University Press: Cambridge, MA), pp. 127–142.

1996. "On Trade-Offs between Values," in Francesco Farina Frank Hahn and Stefano Vannucci (eds.), *Ethics, Rationality and Economic Behaviour* (Clarendon Press: Oxford), pp. 36–49.

Lynn, Laurence E., Carolyn J. Heinrich, and Carolyn J. Hill. 2000. "Studying Governance and Public Management," *Journal of Public Administration Research and Theory*, 10: 233–61.

Macaulay, Michael. 2018. "Ethics and Integrity," in Edoardo Ongaro and Sandra Van Thiel (eds.), *The Palgrave Handbook of Public Administration in Europe* (Palgrave Macmillan: London).

MacIntyre, Alisdair. 1991. *After Virtue* (University of Notre Dame Press: Notre Dame).

Maesschalck, Jeroen. 2004. "The Impact of New Public Management Reforms on Public Servants' Ethics: Towards a Theory," *Public Administration*, 82: 465–89.

March, James, and Johan Olsen. 2006. "The Logic of Appropriateness," in M. Moran, M. Rein, and R. E. Goodin (eds.), *The Oxford Handbook of Public Policy* (Oxford University Press: Oxford), pp. 689–708.

Maynard-Moody, Steven, and Michael Musheno. 2003. *Cops, Teachers, Counselors: Stories from the Front Lines of Public Service* (The University of Michigan Press: Ann-Arbor).

Meijer, Albert, and Jorrit De Jong. 2020. "Managing Value Conflicts in Public Innovation: Ostrich, Chameleon, and Dolphin Strategies," *International Journal of Public Administration*, 43: 977–88.

Meurs, Pauline. 2018. "Situationele gelijkheid: van uniforme normen naar situationele legitimering'." In Van Slingelandt-lezing voor de Vereniging van Bestuurskunde.

Meynhardt, Timo. 2009. "Public Values Inside: What Is Public Values Creation?" *International Journal of Public Administration*, 32: 192–219.

Millgram, Elijah. 1997. "Incommensurability and Practical Reasoning," in Ruth Chang (ed.), *Incommensurability, Incomparability, and Practical Reason* (Harvard University Press: Cambridge, MA), pp. 151–169.

Molina, A. D. 2015. "The Virtues of Administration: Values and the Practice of Public Service," *Administrative Theory and Praxis*, 37: 46–69.

Montefiori, A. 1999. "Integrity: A Philosopher's Introduction," in A. Montefiori and D. Vines (eds.), *Integrity in the Public and Private Domains* (Routledge: London), pp. 3–18.

Moore, M. H. 1995. *Creating Public Value: Strategic Management in Government* (Harvard University Press: Cambridge, MA).

2013. *Recognizing Public Values* (Harvard University Press: Cambridge, MA).

Moran, M. 2003. *The British Regulatory State: High Modernism and Hyper-Innovation* (Oxford University Press: Oxford).

Moulton, Stephanie. 2009. "Putting Together the Publicness Puzzle: A Framework for Realized Publicness," *Public Administration Review*, 69: 889–900.

Nabatchi, T., and M. Leighninger. 2015. *Public Participation for the 21st Century* (Jossey-Bass: Hoboken).

Nederhand, José, Erik-Hans Klijn, Martijn van der Steen, and Mark van Twist. 2018. "The Governance of Self-organization: Which Governance Strategy Do Policy Officials and Citizens Prefer?" *Policy Sciences*, 52: 233–253, Online First.

Nieuwenburg, Paul. 2004. "The Agony of Choice: Isaiah Berlin and the Phenomenology of Conflict," *Administration & Society*, 35: 683–700.

2007. "The Integrity Paradox," *Public Integrity*, 9: 213–24.

2014. "Conflicts of Values and Political Forgivness," *Public Administration Review*, 74: 374–82.

O'Kelly, Ciarán, and Melvin J. Dubnick. 2005. "Taking Tough Choices Seriously: Public Administration and Individual Moral Agency," *Journal of Public Administration Research and Theory*, 16: 393–415.

O'Leary, Rosemary. 2006. *The Ethics of Dissent: Managing Guerrilla Government* (CQ Press: Washington, DC).

Okun, Arthur M. 1975. *Equality and Efficiency: The Big Trade-off* (The Brookings Institution: Washington, DC).

Oldenhof, L., R. Wehrens, and R. Bal. 2022. "Dealing with Conflicting Values in Policy Experiments: A New Pragmatic Approach," *Administration & Society*, 54(9): 1736–1766.

Osborne, Stephen. 2006. 'The New Public Governance?" *Public Management Review*, 8: 377–87.

Osborne, D., and T. Gaebler. 1992. *Reinventing Government: How the Entrepreneurial Spirit is Transforming the Public Sector* (Addison-Wesley: Reading).

Overeem, P. 2011. "After Managerialism: MacIntyre's Lessons for the Study of Public Administration," *Administration & Society*, 43: 722–48.

— 2015. 'The Concept of Regimes Values: Are Revitalization and Regime Change Possible?" *The American Review of Public Administration*, 45: 46–60.

Paanakker, Hester. 2019. "Values of Public Craftsmanship: The Mismatch between Street-Level Ideals and Institutional Facilitation in the Prison Sector," *American Review of Public Administration*, 49: 884–96.

— 2020. *Value Divergence: How Professionals, Managers, and Policy Makers Perceive Public Values and Street-Level Craftmanship in the Prison Sector* (Vrije Universiteit Amsterdam: Amsterdam).

— 2021. "Perceptions of the Frontline Craft: Assessing Value Convergence between Policy Makers, Managers and Street-Level Professionals in the Prison Sector," *Administration & Society*, 53: 222–47.

Page, S. B., M. M. Stone, J. M. Bryson, and B. C. Crosby. 2018. "Coping with Value Conflicts in Interorganizational Collaborations," *Perspectives on Public Management and Governance*, 1: 239–55.

Pesch, Udo. 2005. *The Predicaments of Publicness: An Inquiry into the Conceptual Ambiguity of Public Administration* (Eburon: Delft).

Phillips, N., and C. Hardy. 2002. *Discourse Analysis, Investigating Processes of Social Construction* (Sage: Thousand Oaks).

Powell, M. D., and Michiel S. De Vries. 2011. "The 1990's- Pragmatic Institutionalism: The New Public Management," in O. P. Dwivedi (ed.), *Public Administration in a Global Context: IASIA at 50* (Bruylant: Brussels), pp. 103–133.

Prettner, Robert, Hedwig te Molder, M. Hajer, and Rens Vliegenthart. 2021. "Staging Expertise in Times of COVID-19; An Analysis of the Science-

Policy-Society Interface in the Dutch 'Intelligent Lockdown'," *Frontiers in Communication*, 6: 1–12.

2023. "Light at the End of the Tunnel? The Staging of Expertise during the COVID-19 Vaccination Campaign," *Journal of Digital Social Research*, 5: 140–70.

Provis, Chris. 2007. "Ethics and Issues in Public Policy," *Policy and Society*, 26: 21–33.

Pusey, M. 1991. *Economic Rationalism in Canberra: A Nation-Building State Changes Its Mind* (Cambridge University Press: Sydney).

Putnam, H. 2002. *The Collapse of the Fact/Value Dichotomy and Other Essays* (Harvard University Press: Cambridge, MA).

Putters, K. 2021. *Nieuwe bestuurscultuur begint bij herijking van het sociaal contract. Van Slingelandtlezing* (Sociaal Cultureel Planbureau: Den Haag).

2022a. "Afscheidslezing SCP." www.scp.nl/publicaties/publicaties/2022/06/01/bijlagen-afscheidsbijeenkomst-kim-putters.

2022b. *Het einde van de BV Nederland* (Prometheus: Amsterdam).

Ranchordas, Sofia. 2023. "Empathy in the Digital Administrative State," *Duke Law Journal*, 71: 1341–90.

Ranchordas, Sofia, and Luisa Scarcella. 2021. "Automated Government for Vulnerable Citizens: Intermediating Rights," *William and Mary Bill of Rights Journal*, 30: 373–418.

Raz, Joseph. 1988. *The Morality of Freedom* (Oxford University Press: Oxford).

2005. "The Myth of Instrumental Rationality," *Journal of Ethics and Social Philosophy*, 1: 2–28.

Rein, M. 1976. *Social Science and Public Policy* (Penguin: New York).

Reynaers, A. 2014. "It Takes Two to Tangle: Public-Private Partnerships and Their Impact on Public Values," Vrije Universiteit Amsterdam.

Reynaers, A., and G. de Graaf. 2014. "Public Values in Public-Private Partnerships," *International Journal of Public Administration*, 37: 120–28.

Rhodes, R. A. W. 2007. "Understanding Governance: Ten Years On," *Organization Studies*, 28: 1243–64.

Richardson, H. 1997. *Practical Reasoning about Final Ends* (Cambridge University Press: Cambridge).

Rijksoverheid. 2018. "Klimaatakkoord- H5 Burgerparticipatie," in 73–75.

Ringeling, Arthur. 2017. *Public Administration as a Study of the Public Sphere: A Normative View* (Eleven International: The Hague).

Rohr, J. A. 1989. *Ethics for Bureaucrats: An Essay on Law and Values* (Marcel Dekker: New York).

Rokeach, Milton. 1979. *Understanding Human Values: Individual and Societal* (Free Press: New York).

Rose, R., and P. Davies. 1994. *Inheritance in Public Policy: Change without Choice in Britain* (Yale University Press: New Haven).

Rosenthal, U. 1999. "De politiek-ambtelijke rechtsstaat: Over de tweezijdigheid van de politiek-ambtelijke verhoudingen," *Liberaal Reveil*, 40: 146–51.

Rothstein, Bo, and Jan Teorell. 2008. "What Is the Quality of Government? A Theory of Impartial Government Institutions," *Governance*, 21: 165–90.

Rourke, F. E. 1991. "American Bureaucracy in a Changing Political Setting," *Journal of Public Administration Research and Theory*, 1: 111–29.

Rouwhorst, Zoe. 2022. "De Nederlandse toeslagenaffaire is niet uniek! Een comparatieve casebeschrijving van Noorse, Australische en Nederlandse socialezekerheidsschandalen." Onderzoek-internationale-casusvergelijking-sociale-zekerheid-schandaal-1.pdf

Rutgers, M. R. 2011. *Het pantheon van de publieke waarden* (Oratiereeks Universiteit van Amsterdam: Amsterdam).

2019. "The Rationalities of Public Value: Conflicting Values and Conflicting Rationalities," in A. Lindgreen, N. Koenig-Lewis, M. Kitchener et al. (eds.), *Public Value: Deepening, Enriching, and Broadening the Theory and Practice* (Routledge: Abingdon), pp. 40–52.

Rutgers, Mark. 2015. "As Good as It Gets? On the Meaning of Public Value in the Study of Policy and Management," *American Review of Public Administration*, 45: 29–45.

Sabatier, P., and C. Weible. 2007. "The Advocacy Coalition Framework: Innovations and Clarifications," in P. Sabatier (ed.), *Theories of the Policy Process* (Westview Press: Boulder), pp. 189–220.

Sandel, M. 1996. *Democracy's Discontent: America in Search of Public Philosophy* (Belknap Press: Cambridge).

Schinkel, Willem. 2012. *De nieuwe democratie: Naar andere vormen van politiek* (Klement: Kampen).

Schön, D., and M. Rein. 1994. *Frame Reflection: Toward the Resolution of Intractable Policy* (MIT Press: Boston).

Selden, Sally Coleman, Gene A. Brewer, and Jeffrey L. Brudney. 1999. "Reconciling Competing Values in Public Administration: Understanding the Administrative Role Concept," *Administration & Society*, 31: 171–204.

Self, P. 1982. *Administrative Theories and Politics: An Enquiry into the Structure and Processes of Modern Government* (Allen & Unwin: London).

Selznick, P. 1957. *The Leadership in Administration: A Sociological Interpretation* (McGraw-Hill: New York).

1992. *The Moral Commonwealth: Social Theory and the Promise of Community* (University of California Press: Berkeley).

Sent, Esther-Mirjam. 2014. "Amerikaanse toestanden op Nederlandse universiteiten?" in Ad Verbrugge and Jelle Van Baardewijk (eds.), *Waartoe is de universiteit op aarde?* (Boom: Amsterdam), pp. 95–104.

Sewell, William H. 1992. "A Theory of Structure: Duality, Agency, and Transformation," *The American Journal of Sociology*, 98: 1–29.

Shepsle, Kenneth A. 1979. "Institutional Arrangements and Equilibrium in Multidimensional Voting Models," *American Journal of Political Science*, 23: 27–59.

Simon, Herbert. 1957. *Administrative Behavior: A Study of Decision-Making Processes in Administrative Organization* (Macmillan: New York).

Skolnick, Jerome H. 1967. *Justice without Trial* (John Wiley & Sons: New York).

Smets, Peer, Younes Younes, Marinka Dohmen, Kees Boersma, and Lenie Brouwer. 2017. "Sociale media in en rondom de vluchtelingen-noodopvang bij Nijmegen," *Mens en Maatschappij*, 92: 395–420.

Sørensen, E. 2002. "Democratic Theory and Network Governance," *Administrative Theory & Praxis*, 24: 693–720.

and J. Torfing, 2005. "The Democratic Anchorage of Government Networks," *Scandinavian Political Studies*, 28: 195–218.

2009. "Making Governance Networks Effective and Democratic through Metagovernance," *Public Administration*, 87: 234–58.

2018. "Governance on a Bumpy Road from Enfant Terribke to Mature Paradigm," *Critical Policy Studies*, 12: 350–59.

Spicer, Michael W. 2001. "Value Pluralism and Its Implications for American Public Administration," *Administrative Theory & Praxis*, 23: 507–28.

2005. "Public Administration Enquiry and Social Science in the Postmodern Condition: Some Implications of Value Pluralism," *Administrative Theory & Praxis*, 27: 669–88.

2009. "Value Conflict and Legal Reasoning in Public Administration," *Administrative Theory & Praxis*, 314: 537–55.

2010. *In Defense of Politics: A Value Pluralist Perspective* (The University of Alabama Press: Tuscaloosa).

Starke, A., N. Heckler, and J. Mackey. 2018. "Administrative Racism: Public Administration Education and Race," *Journal of Public Affairs Education*, 24: 469–89.

Steen, Trui, Taco Brandsen, and Bram Verschuere. 2018. "The Dark Side of Co-Creation and Co=Production. Seven Evils," in Taco Brandsen, Trui Steen, and Bram Verschuere (eds.), *Co-Production and Co-Creation* (Routledge: London), pp. 284–93.

Steenhuisen, B. 2009a. "Competing Public Values," *Coping Strategies in Heavily Regulated Utility Industries, Next Generation Infrastructures Dissertation*, Delft.

Steenhuisen, Bauke. 2009b. "Competing Public Values: Coping Strategies in Heavily Regulated Utility Industries," Delft University.

Steenhuisen, Bauke, and Michel van Eeten. 2008. "Invisible Trade-Offs of Public Values: Inside Dutch Railways," *Public Money & Management*, 28: 147–52.

2012. "Patterns of Coping with Inconsistent Demands in Public Service Delivery," *Administration & Society*, 45: 1130–57.

Stewart, Jenny. 2006. "Value Conflict and Policy Change," *Review of Policy Research*, 23: 183–95.

2009. *Public Policy Values* (Palgrave Macmillan: Basingstoke).

Tait, John. 1997. "A Strong Foundation: Report of the Task Force on Public Service Values and Ethics (A Summary)," *Canadian Public Administration*, 40: 1–22.

Talisse, Robert. 2015. "Value Pluralism: A Philosophical Clarification," *Administration & Society*, 47: 1064–79.

Thacher, D., and R. Rein. 2004. "Managing Value Conflict in Public Policy," *Governance*, 17: 457–86.

Thompson, Dennis F. 1985. "The Possibility of Administrative Ethics," *Public Administration Review*, 45: 555–61.

Tjeenk Willink, Herman. 2021. *Kan de overheid crises aan?* (Prometheus: Amsterdam).

Torfing, J., L. Andersen, Carsten Greve, and K. Klausen. 2020. *Public Governance Paradigms: Competing and co-existing* (Edward Elgar: Cheltenham).

Torfing, J., B. Guy Peters, J. Pierre, and E. Sorensen. 2012. *Interactive Governance: Advancing a Paradigm* (Oxford University Press: Oxford).

Trommel, Willem. 2019a. "Good Governance as Reflexive Governance: In Praise of Good Colleagueship," in G. De Graaf (ed.), *It Is All about Integrity, Stupid* (Eleven International Publishing: The Hague), pp. 37–46.

2019b. "Niet meer dan een speldenprik," *Bestuurskunde*, 28: 41–57.

Tummers, Lars, Victor Bekkers, Evelien Vink, and Michael Musheno. 2013. "Handling Stress during Policy Implementation: Developing a Classification of 'Coping' by Frontline Workers Based on a Systematic Overview." In *2013 IRSPM Conference*. Prague.

Twist, M. van. 1994. *Verbale Vernieuwing: Aantekeningen over de Kunst van Bestuurskunde* (Vuga: Den Haag).

Ury, W., J. Brett, and S. Goldberg. 1988. *Getting Disputes Resolved: Designing Systems to Cut the Costs of Conflict* (Jossey-Bass: San Francisco).

Van de Ven, Coen. 2021. "Hoe Den Haag uit Nederland verdween," *De Groene Amsterdammer*, 13 oktober.

Van Der Wal, Z. 2008. "What's Valued Most? Similarities and Differences between the Organizational Values of the Public and Private Sector," *Public Administration*, 86: 465–82.

2016. "Public Values Research in the 21st Century: Where We Are, Where We Haven't Been, and Where We Should Go," *International Journal of Public Administration*, 39: 1–5.

Van der Wal, Z., G. de Graaf, and K. Lasthuizen. 2008. "What's Valued Most? A Comparative Empirical Study on the differences and Similarities between the Organizational Values of the Public and Private Sector," *Public Administration*, 86: 465–82.

Van der Wal, Zeger, Gjalt De Graaf, and Alan Lawton. 2011. "Competing Values in Public Management," *Public Management Review*, 13: 331–41.

Van der Wal, Zeger, Tina Nabatchi, and Gjalt De Graaf. 2015. "From Galaxies to Universe: A Cross-Disciplinary Review and Analysis of Public Values Publications from 1969 to 2012," *American Review of Public Administration*, 45: 13–28.

Van Kersbergen, Kees, and Frans van Waarden. 2004. "'Governance' as a Bridge between Disciplines: Cross-Disciplinary Inspiration Regarding Shifts in Governance and Problems of Governability, Accountability and Empirical Challenges," *European Journal of Political Research*, 43: 143–71.

Van Putten, Robert. 2020. "De ban van beheersing: Naar een felexieve bestuurskunst," Vrije Universiteit Amsterdam.

Van Reybrouck, David. 2013. *Tegen verkiezingen* (Bezige Bij: Amsterdam).

Van Steden, Ronald, Robert Van Putten, and Jan Hoogland. 2019. "Security Networks: Applying the Normative Practice Approach to Nodal Governance Theory," in Marc De Vries and Henk Jochemsen (eds.), *The Normative Nature of Social Practices and Ethics in Professional Environments* (IGI Global: Hershey), pp. 277–94.

Van Wart, Montgomery. 1998. *Changing Public Sector Values* (Garland: Hamden).

Van Wart, Montgomery, and E. Berman. 1999. "Contemporary Public Sector Productivity Values: Narrower Scope, Tougher Standards and New Rules of the Game," *Public Productivity and Management Review*, 22: 326–47.

Voorberg, W. H., V. J. J. M. Bekkers, and L. G. Tummers. 2015. "A Systematic Review of Co-Creation and Co-Production: Embarking on the Social Innovation Journey," *Public Management Review*, 17: 1333–57.

Wagenaar, Hendrik. 1999. "Value Pluralism in Public Administration," *Administrative Theory & Praxis*, 21: 441–49.

Waldo, D. 1984. *The Administrative State: A Study of the Political Theory of American Public Administration* (Holmes & Meier: New York).

Weber, Max. 1946. "Politics as a Vocation," in H. H. Gerth and C. Wright Mills (eds.), *From Max Weber: Essays in Sociology* (Oxford University Press: New York), 26–45.

Weihe, G. 2008. "Public-Private Partnerships and Public-Private Value Trade-Offs," *Public Money & Management*, 28: 153–58.

West, K., and P. Davis. 2011. "What Is the Public Value of Government Action? Towards a (New) Pragmatic Approach to Value Questions in Public Endeavours," *Public Administration*, 89: 226–41.

Whiteford, Peter. 2021. "Debt by Design: The Anatomy of a Social Policy Fiasco – Or Was It Something Worse?" *Australian Journal of Public Administration*, 80: 340–60.

Wildavsky, A. 1983. "Choosing Preferences by Constructing Institutions: A Cultural Theory of Preference Formation," *The American Political Science Review*, 81: 3–22.

Winter, Richard, and Wayne O'Donohue 2012. "Academic Identity Tensions in the Public University: Which Values Really Matter?" *Journal of Higher Education Policy and Management*, 34: 565–73.

Wittgenstein, Ludwig. 2006. *Filosofische Onderzoekingen* (Boom: Amsterdam).

Zacka, Bernardo. 2017. *When the State Meets the Street: Public Service and Moral Agency* (The Belknap Press of Harvard University Press: Cambridge, MA).

2022. "Political Theory Rediscovers Public Administration," *Annual Review of Political Science*, 25: 21–42.

Zavattaro, Staci, Rebeca Entress, Jenna Tyler, and Abdul-Akeem Sadiq. 2021. "When Deaths Are Dehumanized: Deathcare during COVID-19 as a Public Value Failure," *Administration & Society*, 53: 1443–62.

Public and Nonprofit Administration

Robert Christensen
Brigham Young University
Robert Christensen is the George W. Romney Professor of Public and Nonprofit Management at Brigham Young University.

Jaclyn Piatak
University of North Carolina at Charlotte
Jaclyn Piatak is co-editor of NVSQ and Professor of Political Science and Public Administration at the University of North Carolina at Charlotte.

Rosemary O'Leary
University of Kansas
Rosemary O'Leary is the Edwin O. Stene Distinguished Professor Emerita of Public Administration at the University of Kansas.

About the Series
The foundation of this series are cutting-edge contributions on emerging topics and definitive reviews of keystone topics in public and nonprofit administration, especially those that lack longer treatment in textbook or other formats. Among keystone topics of interest for scholars and practitioners of public and nonprofit administration, it covers public management, public budgeting and finance, nonprofit studies, and the interstitial space between the public and nonprofit sectors, along with theoretical and methodological contributions, including quantitative, qualitative and mixed-methods pieces.

The Public Management Research Association
The Public Management Research Association improves public governance by advancing research on public organizations, strengthening links among interdisciplinary scholars, and furthering professional and academic opportunities in public management.

Cambridge Elements

Public and Nonprofit Administration

Elements in the Series

Redefining Development: Resolving Complex Challenges in a Global Context
Jessica Kritz

Experts in Government: The Deep State from Caligula to Trump and Beyond
Donald F. Kettl

New Public Governance as a Hybrid: A Critical Interpretation
Laura Cataldi

Can Governance be Intelligent?: An Interdisciplinary Approach and Evolutionary Modelling for Intelligent Governance in the Digital Age
Eran Vigoda-Gadot

The Courts and the President: Judicial Review of Presidentially Directed Action
Charles Wise

Standing Up for Nonprofits: Advocacy on Federal, Sector-wide Issues
Alan J. Abramson and Benjamin Soskis

Topics in Public Administration: Perspectives from Computational Social Sciences and Corpus Linguistics
Richard M. Walker, Jiasheng Zhang and Yanto Chandra

Public Service Explained: The Role of Citizens in Value Creation
Greta Nasi, Stephen Osborne, Maria Cucciniello and Tie Cui

Court-Ordered Community Service: The Experiences of Community Organizations and Community Service Workers
Rebecca Nesbit, Su Young Choi and Jody Clay-Warner

Sustainable Inclusion through Performance-Driven Practices: An Evidence-Based, Dynamic Systems Framework
Ruth Sessler Bernstein and Paul Salipante

Bureaucratic Resistance in Times of Democratic Backsliding
João V. Guedes-Neto and B. Guy Peters

Value-Based Governance
Gjalt de Graaf

A full series listing is available at: www.cambridge.org/EPNP

For EU product safety concerns, contact us at Calle de José Abascal, 56–1°,
28003 Madrid, Spain or eugpsr@cambridge.org.

www.ingramcontent.com/pod-product-compliance
Lightning Source LLC
LaVergne TN
LVHW011852060526
838200LV00054B/4286